Table of Contents

Pressure Points

Mastering Decision-Making in Life's Critical Moments

by

Dr. ant

Pressure Points: Mastering Decision-Making in Life's Critical Moments

Contents

Chapter 1: Introduction

In the ever-evolving landscape of professional challenges, decision-making stands as a cornerstone skill, crucial to navigating through complexity and uncertainty. We are constantly bombarded with decisions, but those that hold the greatest impact often occur under intense pressure. In these moments, the ability to remain composed and make informed choices becomes our greatest asset. This book aims to guide professionals through the labyrinth of high-pressure decision-making, providing tools and insights to enhance their capabilities in making confident, calculated moves.

When stakes are high, the terrain is rarely predictable. The uncertainty of these scenarios can be daunting, yet they're also opportunities to sharpen our skills and emerge stronger. As we journey through this exploration, think of decision-making not just as a task but as an art form. An art that combines rationality and intuition into a seamless dance, demanding precision, empathy, and courage. Each chapter here will unveil different layers of this intricate process, gradually building a comprehensive framework for you to rely upon.

But why focus on decision-making under pressure, you might wonder? Pressure-induced situations are unique in their ability to strip away the superfluous, demanding clarity and purpose. They make us confront our true selves, often unearthing strengths we might not have recognized. During such times, decisions can define careers and alter life trajectories. Understanding how to navigate these waters is, thus, not just beneficial—it's essential.

In tackling high-stakes scenarios, we must first recognize the elements that contribute to the pressure—these are the pressure points that can sway our judgment. Chapter 2 will delve into understanding and identifying these scenarios, giving you the tools to assess risks and rewards appropriately. The subsequent chapters will build on this foundation, exploring psychological principles, communication strategies, and the role of emotional intelligence.

Picture a leader, standing on the precipice of a crucial choice, where every decision will ripple across their organization. Imagine the level of calm and clarity required to make such a choice effectively. This calmness is a result of preparation, understanding, and a well-practiced decision-making framework. This book serves as both a guide and a companion, equipping you with proven strategies and practical tips to enhance your decision-making prowess.

Confidence in decision-making doesn't come from knowing all the answers but from trusting one's ability to navigate through uncertainty. This book fosters that trust. By learning from leaders across various fields, you'll discover methods to incorporate into your own decision-making style. Whether it's insights from military strategies or the adaptability seen in emergency services, there's much to learn from others' experiences that can be tailored to suit your unique context.

Moreover, today's world offers multifaceted tools to aid our decisions. From data analytics to AI-powered assessments, technology stands as a formidable ally. Yet, while these resources are powerful, they must be complemented with human judgment and ethics—topics we'll explore further. We'll emphasize creating a balanced approach, ensuring decisions based on data are ethically grounded and human-centric.

As we commence this journey together, I encourage you to approach it with an open mind and a willingness to be introspective. Understanding your decision-making tendencies and biases is the first step towards mastery. Be prepared to challenge existing patterns and embrace new strategies, ensuring that when high-pressure moments arise, you respond with agility and assurance.

Ultimately, this book is about empowerment. It's about crafting a mindset that is not just reactive but strategic, foreseeing potential obstacles and opportunities before they manifest. By blending theory with real-world application, you'll emerge not only as a more capable decision-maker but as a leader poised to influence and inspire others in times of adversity.

Let's transform the art of decision-making into an exhilarating pursuit, one that enhances your professional capabilities and allows you to thrive under any circumstances. Welcome to a journey that promises growth and resilience, where each decision you make builds a bridge to a brighter, more decisive future.

Chapter 2: Understanding Pressure Points

To navigate the complex world of high-stakes decision-making, understanding pressure points is crucial. These moments often define our professional journeys, testing not only our strategic acumen but also our ability to stay composed under stress. Recognizing these situations quickly involves analyzing the stakes at hand and discerning patterns of emotional and cognitive responses they trigger. It's here that professionals find their resilience challenged, calling for a balance between swift judgments and calculated risk assessments. By identifying these critical junctures, individuals can transform pressure into a catalyst for improved performance. Whether in boardrooms or crisis management scenarios, awareness of pressure points empowers leaders to make informed choices, harnessing stress not as a constraint but as a source of strategic advantage. Embracing this perspective encourages a mindset shift, steering us toward growth and fortified decision-making capabilities, all of which are essential as we build a framework for managing uncertainty with clarity and confidence.

Recognizing High-Stakes Scenarios

In the fast-paced environment that defines today's professional world, the capacity to identify high-stakes scenarios is crucial. These are not your everyday decisions. High-stakes scenarios involve those pivotal moments where choices bear significant impact, either paving the way for transformative gains or casting shadows of substantial losses. Recognizing such scenarios is a vital skill for anyone seeking to hone their decision-making prowess. It demands more than just experience; it requires acute awareness, astute perception, and the ability to discern subtle cues amid the noise of daily operations.

What turns an ordinary decision into a high-stakes scenario? It's often the convergence of several factors: the potential consequences of the decision, the time pressure involved, and the spotlight under which the decision must be made. Imagine a CEO deciding whether to merge with another company, a doctor diagnosing a complex case, or a military leader strategizing in the face of imminent conflict. These instances demand more than routine analysis; they necessitate a deep dive into the ramifications of each possible choice.

Consider a financial manager facing a volatile market. Here, the stakes are not only measured by potential financial gains or losses but also by the ripple effects on clients, the firm's reputation, and even the broader economic environment. Recognizing high-stakes scenarios involves identifying these ripple effects—understanding how a decision can transcend its immediate context and reverberate through interconnected networks.

To cultivate this recognition skill, professionals must first develop an awareness of external pressures—those originating from market dynamics, competitive landscapes, and organizational hierarchies. Equally important is the internal landscape: emotions, biases, and personal principles also shape how we perceive stakes. The interplay of these internal and external factors can obscure clarity, necessitating a mindset attuned to distinguishing the trivial from the consequential.

Take, for example, the challenge of time sensitivity. High-stakes scenarios often come cloaked in time constraints, compressing the decision-making window and heightening the intensity of the situation. Leaders must swiftly weigh options, with no luxury for prolonged deliberation. The pressure-cooker environment amplifies the need to recognize these inflection points acutely, where timing is as much a decisive factor as the decision itself.

Developing the capability to recognize high-stakes scenarios begins with rigorous self-assessment. Professionals must question their own readiness to differentiate significant moments from routine ones. Self-awareness acts as the bedrock of discernment. It includes understanding personal thresholds for risk tolerance and emotional triggers that might cloud judgment in critical times.

The next stride is building a framework of criteria that signals when stakes are indeed high. Criteria can include potential financial implications, ethical considerations, stakeholder interests, and more. This scaffolding helps filter through the noise, allowing decision-makers to prioritize correctly without getting derailed by every apparent urgent issue. By establishing clear markers of significance, we create a roadmap that guides our attention toward what truly matters.

Furthermore, enhancing situational awareness through continual learning and observation equips us with insights into how high-stakes scenarios present themselves across various contexts. Studying past cases, both of success and failure, enriches our repository of knowledge. It helps prepare for future challenges. Real-world examples offer lessons in foresight and hindsight, illustrating how others have navigated the choppy waters of complex decisions. Through these narratives, we gain perspectives that refine our instincts.

In recognizing high-stakes scenarios, intuition and analysis go hand in hand. Intuition acts as a radar, swiftly alerting us to potential importance based on patterns and experiences. Yet, it must be tempered with analytical rigor to verify gut feelings with data and evidence. This synergy between intuition and analysis ensures that neither is over reliant—a balanced approach that bolsters confidence in discerning when the stakes are, indeed, high.

To foster this ability, practicing scenario planning is invaluable. By visualizing a range of possible outcomes and their implications before they manifest, professionals can train themselves to identify potential high-stakes situations ahead of time. Such proactive preparation serves as a mental rehearsal, sharpening recognition skills and enhancing readiness when reality presents similar challenges.

Emphasizing collaboration further strengthens our capacity to recognize high-stakes scenarios. Diverse teams bring varied experiences, perspectives, and cognitive styles to the table, collectively enriching the decision-making process. When individuals pool their insights, they create a more comprehensive picture that aides in accurately pinpointing scenarios where the stakes are elevated. It's the diversity of thought that sharpens collective perception.

Finally, embracing a mindset that is open to adaptability and change is paramount. High-stakes situations often arise from unexpected twists and turns; flexibility enables professionals to pivot and respond effectively. Recognizing the high stakes is just the first step; being agile enough to adapt strategies in the face of fresh information or evolving circumstances is where true decision-making mastery is realized.

In summary, recognizing high-stakes scenarios is an essential precursor to confident decision-making. It's about fine-tuning our senses to detect when ordinary scales tip into the extraordinary. Through self-awareness, criteria development, continuous learning, and collaboration, professionals are better prepared to spot these critical moments. By doing so, they position themselves to approach each decision with clarity, courage, and the conviction needed to navigate high-stakes environments successfully.

Assessing Risks and Rewards

Understanding the pressure points in decision-making is akin to dissecting a complex equation with numerous variables, each holding potential for impact. At its core, assessing risks and rewards is about finding balance, a delicate dance between acknowledging potential downsides and still pushing forward toward opportunity. This balance is not only crucial in high-stakes situations but also in everyday decisions where precision is required.

In high-pressure scenarios, the stakes are elevated, and the outcomes are amplified, which makes the ability to accurately assess risks and rewards all the more critical. It's not merely about listing the pros and cons, but delving deeper into the likelihood of each outcome and their potential repercussions. Successful decision-makers are often those who can intuitively, or through calculated consideration, weigh these elements against each other. They possess a knack for judging whether the glory of potential success outweighs the haunting consequences of failure.

The process begins with identifying all possible risks. These aren't just the obvious or immediate threats. It's essential to screen for hidden traps that might lay in the shadows, awaiting the right conditions to spring forth. Risks in decision-making can be financial, reputational, or even ethical. The uncertainty surrounding these risks often stems from an array of intrinsic and extrinsic factors that can alter the landscape in a heartbeat.

Next, effective decision-makers map out potential rewards with the same vigor. Rewards, unlike risks, often appear alluring, whispering promises of glory, profit, or advancement. However, outperforming at this stage requires an objective evaluation of these rewards by posing critical questions: Are they realistic? Do they align with broader goals and values? Do they offer sustainable benefits or are they merely short-term fixes?

There's an art to balancing the quantitative analysis with qualitative judgment. Data and analytics provide invaluable insights into the probability and impact of various outcomes. Yet, while data-driven approaches anchor our understanding, it is through intuitive insight that we grasp complexities that numbers alone cannot encapsulate. Ideally, a thorough risk-versus-reward assessment integrates quantitative modeling with qualitative forecasting.

A pivotal element in this assessment is understanding personal risk tolerance and how that meshes with the stakes at hand. Risk tolerance is inherently personal, shaped by past experiences, confidence levels, and even emotional states. Developing a decision-making framework hinges on being authentic to one's comfort zone while challenging oneself to edge just beyond it in pursuit of growth.

Furthermore, weighing risks and rewards must also account for timing. Timing can transform a project set for shambles into a roaring success, or vice-versa. A calculated delay might allow for better conditions whereas seizing a narrowly-timed opportunity might preclude a competitor from gaining ground.

Assessing risks and rewards also involves expecting and planning for unexpected turns. Contingency plans become the safety nets for ventures into unknown territories. Leaders and decision-makers must train their minds to anticipate different "what if" scenarios, creating robust plans that can withstand variability in outcomes.

Equally important is the use of feedback loops post-decision. Establishing mechanisms to evaluate the repercussions of decisions aids in refining future judgments. Retrospective analysis should assess whether the anticipated risks and rewards matched reality and, if not, investigate why discrepancies occurred. This reflective practice is vital for honing a sharp decision-making acumen.

In instances where risks appear to overshadow rewards, decision-makers must sometimes embrace boldness. Fortitude in the face of adversity can convert potential liabilities into strengths. For instance, leveraging a seemingly high-risk situation for innovation can yield unforeseen rewards, exemplifying the potential for creative problem-solving under pressure.

Yet, there are ethical implications intertwined in risk and reward assessment. Decisions at the pressure point should lucidly align with personal and organizational values, maintaining integrity even in arduous circumstances. The ethical calculus forms a silent undercurrent in every decision where risks intersect with rewards, ensuring choices honor greater societal and organizational responsibility.

In an ensemble of these factors, assessing risks and rewards doesn't conclude with strategies and analytical techniques alone. It demands a mindset; a shift to view challenges with a lens that captures not only the complexities but also the simplicity of ambition. This mindset encourages courage, a relentless pursuit of improvement, and a deep commitment to principled leadership.

Ultimately, the assessment of risks and rewards in decision-making is a journey towards clarity in chaos, providing a compass that guides through ambiguity. It's about leveraging knowledge and intuition, understanding timing and timing yet again, and holding steadfast to values and ethics. This mastery becomes the cornerstone upon which decisions can safely and effectively be built, even when the stakes are towering.

Chapter 3: The Psychology of Decision-Making Under Pressure

In the intense arena of high-pressure decision-making, understanding the psychological forces at play is crucial to achieving clarity and confidence. Under stress, our brains naturally resort to shortcuts and biases, often clouding judgment at critical moments. Recognizing these cognitive biases not only helps mitigate their impact but also sharpens our ability to make more rational choices under pressure. Moreover, cultivating emotional intelligence allows professionals to remain composed and focused, transforming stress from a hindrance into a compelling catalyst for decisive action. By adopting a mindset that embraces this dual understanding of psychology and emotion, individuals can navigate high-stakes scenarios with increased precision and agility. This chapter offers insights into harnessing these psychological dynamics, empowering decision-makers to thrive when the stakes are highest.

Cognitive Biases and Their Impact

Human decision-making is a fascinating amalgam of rational thought and emotional influence, often producing outcomes that defy straightforward logic. In high-pressure situations, the role of cognitive biases becomes particularly pronounced, subtly skewing our perception and choices. These biases, deeply ingrained in our psyche, don't just lurk in the shadows; they shape the very way we interpret and act upon information. Understanding these biases is crucial for professionals who want to make more informed, confident decisions under stress.

Cognitive biases are essentially systematic deviations from rationality. They're the mind's shortcuts, think of them as heuristics that simplify complex decision-making processes. While these can be helpful in quickly assessing options and reaching decisions, they often lead us astray, particularly under pressure. Take, for instance, the confirmation bias — a tendency to favor information that confirms our pre-existing beliefs. This bias can trap decision-makers into echo chambers, reinforcing flawed strategies or overlooking innovative solutions simply because they challenge the status quo.

The anchoring effect is another such bias, where initial information serves as a reference point and unduly influences subsequent judgments. In high-stakes environments, where every second counts, decisions can be disproportionately affected by initial perceptions or information, leading to suboptimal choices. Picture a negotiation where the first offer dictates the range for all future discussions, even if irrelevant to the actual value at stake. Recognizing the anchoring effect enables decision-makers to question starting points and consider a broader spectrum of possibilities.

One might also encounter the availability heuristic, which leans on the most immediate examples that come to mind. In high-pressure scenarios, this can result in overestimating the importance of recent information or dramatic events, skewing risk assessments. For professionals, especially those in leadership roles, it is critical to balance the vivid, easily recalled events with a more systematic analysis of all available data, ensuring that decisions are grounded in reality rather than cognitive illusion.

Emotional states, particularly anxiety and stress, can exacerbate cognitive biases. Under duress, individuals might experience heightened feelings of loss aversion — a bias that places a greater emphasis on avoiding losses over acquiring gains. This bias can lead to overly conservative decisions that discount innovative opportunities. For a leader, recognizing this tendency can be pivotal in steering teams away from an excessive focus on risk elimination towards a more balanced consideration of potential rewards.

Now, consider the bandwagon effect, where the probability of adopting a belief increases based on the rate of its adoption by others. In the crucible of high-pressure decision-making, the fear of standing out often leads professionals to conform to popular opinion, stifling creativity and disregarding diverse perspectives. Challenging this bias involves fostering an environment where dissenting opinions are valued and explored, providing a more rounded perspective on the scenario at hand.

Another subtle yet potent bias is the overconfidence bias, characterized by an inflated sense of one's knowledge or ability. In high-stakes decision-making, particularly in volatile markets or crisis situations, overconfidence can blind professionals to risks and alternative strategies. The antidote to this bias is cultivating a mindset of intellectual humility—acknowledging the limits of one's knowledge and actively seeking out, and considering, contrasting viewpoints. Encouraging a culture where questions are welcomed and uncertainties are discussed can counterbalance this bias.

The hindsight bias, often referred to as the "I-knew-it-all-along" effect, can impact learning from past decisions. When evaluating the outcome of decisions made under pressure, professionals may reinterpret past events as having been more predictable than they actually were. This bias can obstruct genuine learning by masking the complexity and unpredictability inherent in high-stakes decision-making processes. Acknowledging hindsight bias fosters a more nuanced understanding of past decisions, aiding in future preparedness.

Furthermore, the sunk cost fallacy, where individuals continue an endeavor once an investment in money, effort, or time has been made, often clouds judgment. In pressure-laden environments, this fallacy can compel professionals to persist with failing strategies simply because they are reluctant to "waste" previously allocated resources. The key to overcoming this bias lies in focusing on current and future outcomes rather than past expenses—an approach that leads to more objective and strategic decision-making.

Mitigating the impact of cognitive biases requires deliberate effort and conscious strategies. Developing a habit of critical questioning and self-reflection can significantly reduce the influence of biases. Adopting a structured decision-making framework allows professionals to step back and assess options from multiple angles, reducing impulsivity. Tools such as decision trees, pros and cons lists, and pre-mortem analysis can help clarify thinking and affirm well-rounded decisions.

Incorporating diverse perspectives into decision-making processes also serves as a strong defense against cognitive biases. Diverse teams offer a mosaic of insights and counterpoints that can challenge entrenched biases and reinforce sound judgment. Encouraging open dialogue, fostering a culture that values differing views, and promoting active engagement with dissenting opinions nurture an environment where cognitive biases are less likely to flourish.

Emotional intelligence plays a complementary role in understanding and counteracting biases. Developing awareness of one's emotional triggers and their impact on decision-making sharpens the ability to remain focused and logical under pressure. Mindfulness practices and stress management techniques can help maintain a calm demeanor, supporting more objective evaluation and planning.

Finally, fostering a growth mindset encourages continuous learning and adaptation in the face of cognitive biases. Recognizing that biases are natural human tendencies rather than personal failings enables professionals to approach them with curiosity rather than defensiveness. By embracing the idea that decision-making is a skill that can be refined over time, individuals build resilience and adaptability, essential traits for navigating today's ever-changing high-pressure landscapes.

Recognizing and mitigating cognitive biases is not an overnight task, but a lifelong journey. It's a quest for greater awareness, deeper understanding, and enhanced decision-making capacity. As we peel back the layers of bias and its impact on decision-making under pressure, we uncover not just the limitations of our thinking, but also the potential for growth and improvement. By consciously addressing these biases, professionals can cultivate more effective strategies for decision-making, leading to better outcomes for themselves and their organizations.

Emotional Intelligence in Critical Moments

In high-pressure situations, the ability to navigate through emotions isn't just beneficial—it's essential. Emotional intelligence, often abbreviated as EI, forms the backbone of effective decision-making when the stakes are high. At its core, emotional intelligence involves understanding and managing your own emotions, as well as empathizing with others' feelings. When pressure mounts and the clock ticks, those with strong EI can maintain composure, lead with clarity, and make confident decisions without being clouded by stress or anxiety.

Imagine you're in a boardroom, about to make a pivotal decision that could impact your company for years. The data is ambiguous, and the team is divided. At this moment, EI helps you identify and regulate any personal biases or anxieties that may affect your judgment. It allows you to process feedback from others without defensiveness, ensuring that their inputs are genuinely considered. In such scenarios, emotional intelligence isn't just about controlling emotions—it's about leveraging them to enhance understanding and drive better outcomes.

Emotional intelligence in decision-making isn't just an abstract concept—it's a practical tool rooted in self-awareness. By recognizing how your emotions affect your thoughts and actions, you can identify patterns in your decision-making process that may either help or hinder you. For instance, if you notice your judgments are consistently swayed by stress, you can take proactive steps to mitigate this influence. It might be as straightforward as taking a deep breath before a meeting or as complex as restructuring the decision process to involve input from an emotionally balanced colleague.

But emotional intelligence goes beyond self-awareness. It involves an acute understanding of social awareness, where empathy and active listening become vital. Imagine trying to rally your team for a last-minute project. If you're tuned in to their emotional states, you can craft a message that resonates and motivates rather than dictating orders that may provoke resistance. This is particularly critical in high-stakes environments, where team buy-in can be the dividing line between success and failure.

Building emotional intelligence takes practice. Start by reflecting on recent decisions and assessing how emotions played a role. Were there moments when your stress or excitement clouded your judgment? Did you miss out on valuable perspectives from colleagues by letting your emotions guide you? By acknowledging these instances, you can begin to recalibrate your approach, cultivating a heightened sensitivity to both your emotional state and those around you.

As you hone your emotional intelligence, it's helpful to remember that emotions aren't the enemy of reason. Instead, they are powerful data sources that provide insights into what truly matters to you and your colleagues. For example, if a decision feels particularly hard, it might be because it's touching on deeply held values or concerns. Recognizing this can guide you to make decisions that are not only pragmatic but also align with your core principles.

While developing strong EI is beneficial on a personal level, its advantages multiply in a team setting. In collaborative environments, emotionally intelligent leaders can transform how groups interact and make decisions. They make space for different viewpoints, recognizing that diverse emotions and perspectives enrich the decision-making process. This diversity can lead to more innovative solutions, as varied experiences and insights are woven into the final decision.

Moreover, emotional intelligence helps manage conflict. In high-pressure situations, disagreements may arise, fueled by stress and differing opinions. Armed with EI, decision-makers can address these conflicts constructively, fostering a culture where emotions are acknowledged and respected. This doesn't only help resolve the immediate issue but also builds a foundation of trust and collaboration for future challenges.

Ultimately, emotional intelligence is about adaptability. When decisions don't go as planned—which is inevitable—being emotionally intelligent means you can pivot gracefully, taking setbacks in stride and reframing them as learning opportunities. This resilience is crucial, especially when previous decisions cast a long shadow over current circumstances. Recognizing and regulating disappointment or fear allows for clearer reflection on what went wrong and how to move forward.

To cultivate emotional intelligence, consider integrating mindfulness practices into your daily routine. Mindfulness can enhance your emotional awareness, helping you observe your thoughts and feelings without judgment. This clarity aids in identifying how emotions influence your decisions and interactions. Pair it with regular feedback from peers and mentors, focusing on how your emotional responses impact your leadership and decision-making abilities.

Additionally, training programs and workshops on emotional intelligence can provide structured learning paths, equipping you with theoretical knowledge and practical exercises. These opportunities provide a platform for self-discovery and personal growth, fostering the skills that define an emotionally intelligent leader capable of making sound decisions under pressure.

In conclusion, emotional intelligence doesn't just affect decisions made in critical moments—it defines them. By developing this set of skills, you transform how you approach challenges, leading with empathy and understanding rather than reacting impulsively. As pressure becomes a constant companion in your professional journey, emotional intelligence ensures that you navigate it with confidence, clarity, and conviction, making decisions that stand the test of time.

Chapter 4: Developing a Decision-Making Framework

In the heart of high-pressure environments, a steadfast decision-making framework serves as both compass and anchor. It begins with the establishment of core values and principles, guiding lights that steadfastly illuminate the path through complex challenges. Imagine building a personal model where each decision aligns with these values, fostering consistently sound choices. By meticulously crafting a framework, you're equipping yourself with a reliable toolset, capable of evolving yet grounded in guiding principles. This structured approach acts not only as a shield against cognitive biases but also as a catalyst for confidence, providing clarity and direction amidst the chaos. This chapter delves into the essence of such frameworks, inviting you to construct a personal methodology tailored to withstand the test of any high-stakes scenario you may encounter.

Establishing Core Values and Principles

Developing a robust decision-making framework starts with a deep understanding of one's core values and principles. These are the bedrocks upon which every decision rests. They serve as guiding stars when the path forward is murky and the stakes are high. By establishing these foundational beliefs, we create a compass that not only directs us in moments of pressure but also aligns our actions with our personal and professional integrity.

Core values are the fundamental beliefs and standards that shape how individuals conduct themselves, both personally and professionally. They are the principles that individuals aren't willing to compromise, even when faced with daunting challenges. Establishing these values requires introspection and honesty. It's about identifying what truly matters, beyond external accolades or immediate gains. These values might be integrity, accountability, or innovation, but they need to resonate deeply with the individual's authentic self.

Having clear principles is essential for consistent decision-making. While decisions made under pressure can sometimes lead to ethical quandaries or shortcuts, adhering to established values ensures that one remains true to their commitments and moral compass. This is crucial in maintaining trust with colleagues, stakeholders, and oneself. When values are clear, decisions naturally align with both short-term goals and long-term visions.

However, identifying these core values is just the beginning. The real challenge lies in embedding them into the organizational culture and daily decision-making processes. This requires active reflection and regular dialogue within teams to ensure alignment with shared principles. It's a process of translating personal values into communal norms, fostering an environment where individuals feel empowered and accountable to act according to mutually respected standards.

As we navigate high-pressure environments, it's crucial to embrace the clarity that comes from well-defined values. When confronted with complex decisions, these values act as filters that help prioritize actions and streamline choices. They serve as anchors in turbulent times, enabling us to persevere with purpose rather than be swayed by external pressures or fleeting trends.

It's also beneficial to periodically revisit and refine our core values. The world is dynamic, and so are we. As we grow and our circumstances evolve, our values might shift. Regular reflection ensures that we remain aligned with our true selves, while also adapting to new insights and experiences. This doesn't mean changing values capriciously but rather integrating growth and learning into our foundational beliefs.

Moreover, establishing core values tangentially impacts decision-making by fostering resilience. When we are steadfast in our values, setbacks become easier to manage. Challenges are reframed not as barriers but as opportunities to test and affirm our principles. This resilience cultivates a mindset that can handle pressure with grace and determination, knowing that choices made are in alignment with core beliefs.

In high-stakes scenarios, where emotions can run high and cognitive biases may skew perception, having a set of core principles to rely on acts as a calming influence. They remind us of the larger picture, enabling us to navigate through immediate distractions and stay focused on strategic goals. This focus enhances decision-making effectiveness by reducing noise and clarifying what truly matters in the moment.

Furthermore, establishing core values and principles facilitates better communication and collaboration within teams. When team members are aligned with shared values, discussions become more productive and less conflicted. There's a shared language and understanding, which helps in resolving disputes and reaching consensus. This alignment lays the groundwork for trust, an essential component in any effective decision-making environment.

To anchor values effectively within a decision-making framework, it's vital to consider them during the planning stage of any project or initiative. Before diving into strategy or implementation details, taking time to reflect on how core values intersect with objectives can yield significant benefits. This practice ensures that values are not just theoretical ideals but are actively integrated at every stage of decision-making.

Encouraging a culture where core values are explicitly discussed and emphasized leads to collective ownership and accountability. When everyone understands and commits to shared values, decision-making becomes more fluid and coherent. This sense of unity is invaluable, especially when facing unpredictable challenges, as it assures that everyone is working towards the same vision with unwavering commitment.

In conclusion, establishing core values and principles within a decision-making framework is more than just an exercise in introspection. It's an ongoing journey of aligning one's personal beliefs with actions, creating consistency and clarity in the face of pressure. These values act as silent yet powerful mentors, guiding us through the complexities of decision-making with integrity and purpose. As we evolve, so too must our understanding of these values, ensuring they continue to illuminate our path towards confident and informed choices. By prioritizing these foundational elements, we equip ourselves with the resilience and clarity needed to navigate the high-stakes decisions that define our professional and personal journeys.

Creating a Personal Decision-Making Model

In the journey of enhancing decision-making under pressure, creating a personal decision-making model can serve as a pivotal turn. It's where theory meets practice, where your unique insights and experiences coalesce into a framework that is not only tailored to your strengths but also designed to mitigate your weaknesses. This is not a one-size-fits-all solution. It's an invitation for introspection, challenging you to scrutinize your own patterns and biases. After all, who knows your decision-making habits better than you?

Imagine for a moment the components of a reliable model. It should seamlessly integrate the knowledge of your core values, learned principles, and past experiences. The idea here is not about forcing a rigid structure on spontaneous decisions but rather building a flexible support system that adapts to various high-stakes environments. At its heart, a personal model is about guiding yourself to make consistently sound choices while embracing the fluidity of uncertain situations.

Begin by establishing a foundation with your core values and principles. Identify what drives you, what you cannot compromise on—your non-negotiables. This moral compass becomes your anchor in stormy seas. With these values clearly in mind, you'll establish a clearer direction, even when decisions become tough. Reflect on occasions where these values might have been tested. How did you respond? What could you learn from those moments to inform your future actions?

Next, delve into the process of decision-making itself. Understanding your cognitive biases is crucial. These mental shortcuts, while sometimes helpful, often lead us astray under pressure. Combatting them demands a keen awareness of their presence and effect. Developing methods to slow down and critically evaluate situations can help dissipate the haze of bias. Challenging assumptions and inviting alternative viewpoints are steps towards unveiling the deeper truths obscured by cognitive fog.

Incorporating emotional intelligence is another essential component of a personal decision-making model. How do emotions shape your decisions? Emotional intelligence equips you to recognize, understand, and manage how you feel under duress. It's not about suppressing emotions but rather using them to your advantage. Balancing logic and emotion allows for decisions that resonate with both the head and the heart, enhancing the ability to act confidently even in high-stakes scenarios.

This model should also include a method for evaluating risks and rewards. Weighing these factors against the backdrop of your goals and values ensures that decisions align with your broader vision. Every choice carries inherent risks, but assessing them with a clear-headed view can transform potential pitfalls into opportunities for growth and learning. Risk assessment isn't about seeking zero risk but managing it effectively to a level you find acceptable.

Moreover, consider how you'll incorporate feedback loops into your model. Effective decision-making doesn't happen in a vacuum. Gathering input from trusted colleagues or mentors and reflecting on outcomes is invaluable. Learn to recognize and extract constructive criticism and be open to adapting your model based on what you learn. Utilize each scenario as an education opportunity, further refining how you approach future decisions under pressure.

An aspect often overlooked in personal decision-making models is time management. A solid model recognizes that time is a finite resource that can influence the quality of decisions. Developing strategies to manage time efficiently, prioritize tasks, and maintain focus under pressing circumstances is crucial. When time constraints are part of the equation, techniques for rapid decision-making become indispensable tools.

Your personal decision-making model should remain a living document. It's not set in stone but should evolve as you grow and as your environment changes. Flexibility is key, enabling you to adapt to new challenges proactively. Revisit and revise your model periodically to ensure it remains relevant and aligned with your evolving professional objectives.

As you craft and refine your model, be mindful of its application in group settings. While this personal model is uniquely yours, understanding how to integrate it within team dynamics is invaluable. Recognizing the models of others and blending them harmoniously can lead to more effective and cohesive team decisions. Collaboration doesn't mean compromising your model; rather, it means leveraging the diversity of approaches for a better outcome.

In conclusion, creating a personal decision-making model is about empowering yourself with a tailored framework that provides clarity and confidence amid the sweeping chaos of high-pressure environments. It's a dynamic guide that respects your values, constrains biases, harnesses emotional intelligence, and embraces adaptability. With this model, your decisions are no longer just reactions to immediate pressures but thoughtful responses to complex and evolving scenarios.

Chapter 5: Learning from Leadership

In the fast-paced world of decision-making, leadership provides a rich tapestry of insights to guide us. Leaders often stand at the crossroads of choice, where every decision can ripple through an organization or, indeed, the world. It's from those who've walked these high-pressure paths that we can draw valuable lessons. By examining the approaches of successful leaders—whether from the business arena or military landscapes—we gain a nuanced understanding of focus, adaptability, and conviction. These leaders teach us that at the core of effective decision-making lies not just strategy, but a steadfast adherence to one's principles and values. Their experiences remind us that while data and models provide crucial support, authentic leadership in decision-making springs from a willingness to take responsibility and learn continuously. Recognizing this amalgam of courage and reflection can help each of us refine our decision-making skills, ensuring we stand better prepared for the inevitable high-stakes decisions of our own lives.

Business Leaders' Decision-Making Insights

Business leaders are often faced with decisions that can make or break an organization. Their ability to navigate these high-stakes moments with clarity and foresight is what sets them apart and offers valuable lessons for others. One key insight is the importance of maintaining a balance between data-driven analysis and intuitive judgment. Leaders understand that while data provides a foundation for decision-making, it is their experience and instincts that often guide them in the right direction when facing ambiguous situations.

The complexities of modern business challenges mean that leaders must develop a robust decision-making framework that's flexible enough to adapt to varying circumstances. This involves setting core values and principles as a compass, allowing them to navigate through the fog of uncertainty. When leaders align their decisions with their foundational values, they maintain consistency and integrity, fostering trust within their organizations.

Furthermore, business leaders recognize the significance of a diverse perspective. In critical decision-making moments, they gather insights from a wide range of voices within their organizations. This practice not only enriches the decision-making process but also minimizes blind spots that can arise from a singular point of view. Leaders understand that diverse teams bring varied experiences and ideas, which can lead to innovative solutions that might not have emerged otherwise.

Leaders also emphasize the importance of agility in decision-making. In today's rapidly changing business environment, prolonged deliberation can result in missed opportunities. Therefore, leaders cultivate a mindset that embraces change and uncertainty, viewing them as opportunities for growth rather than threats. They know that adapting quickly to new information can create a competitive advantage, allowing them to stay ahead of industry shifts.

Moreover, successful business leaders are adept at managing ambiguity and complexity. They develop the ability to distill complex information into actionable insights, which simplifies decision-making under pressure. This skill involves identifying the most critical variables that impact desired outcomes and focusing resources on them. By doing so, they can streamline decision-making processes and enhance operational efficiency.

Communication plays a crucial role in the decision-making process. Effective leaders ensure that their communication is transparent, aligning teams with their strategic vision. They articulate the rationale behind decisions, ensuring that everyone understands the goals and expectations. This not only aligns the organization but also empowers individuals to take initiative, fostering a culture of accountability and innovation.

Resilience in the face of setbacks is another critical trait observed in top business leaders. Decisive action doesn't always mean infallibility; mistakes are bound to happen. However, it's the ability to learn from these experiences, recalibrate, and drive forward that defines outstanding leadership. Leaders use setbacks as learning opportunities, harnessing them to refine their decision-making frameworks and strategies.

Through continuous learning and improvement, leaders stay ahead of the curve. They invest in their own development and encourage their teams to do the same. This commitment to growth creates an environment where individuals are constantly enhancing their skills, pushing boundaries, and challenging the status quo. It's this relentless pursuit of excellence that equips organizations to navigate high-stakes decisions with confidence.

Another noteworthy insight is the role of ethical considerations in decision-making. Leaders recognize that ethical dilemmas are prevalent in high-pressure situations, and they prioritize long-term integrity over short-term gains. By doing so, they uphold the values and reputation of their organizations, ensuring sustainable growth and success.

Finally, business leaders demonstrate the importance of building and nurturing networks. By cultivating a community of trusted advisors and peers, they create a support system that provides diverse perspectives and valuable feedback. This network acts as a sounding board, enhancing their ability to make informed decisions and reinforcing their commitment to strategic objectives.

In conclusion, business leaders offer profound insights into effective decision-making under pressure. By integrating data with intuition, embracing diversity, prioritizing ethical standards, and fostering open communication, they navigate the complexities of their environments with resilience and adaptability. Their experiences not only illuminate the path to success but also empower others to refine their own decision-making skills, driving personal and organizational excellence.

Military Approaches to High-Stakes Decisions

History's battlegrounds offer a unique and powerful lens through which to understand decision-making in high-stakes scenarios. In the military, the stakes couldn't be higher: lives hang in the balance, and the outcomes can alter the course of nations. Military leaders have not only been tasked with devising strategies under intense pressure but have also had to learn quickly from each decision made on the field. Their approaches to decision-making provide profound lessons for anyone seeking to improve their skills under pressure. These methodologies, honed over centuries, illustrate the art and science of making swift, yet calculated choices.

The first key insight from military decision-making is the importance of preparation and strategy. Military leaders plan meticulously, often considering a range of scenarios before an operation is even launched. This level of preparation allows them to remain flexible and adaptive as events unfold. Drawing parallels to the business world, detailed planning and scenario analysis can be just as vital. Dwight D. Eisenhower, a prominent military leader and U.S. president, once remarked that, "Plans are useless, but planning is indispensable." This underscores the value of the planning process itself to prepare decision-makers for whatever comes their way.

One cannot overlook the role of experience in refining decision-making skills. Military leaders undergo rigorous training designed to simulate high-pressure environments, allowing them to practice and refine their responses to stress. This intensive training builds a foundation of experience and confidence, enabling leaders to act decisively when seconds matter. For professionals outside the military, this serves as a reminder of the value of experiential learning. Those in leadership positions can benefit from engaging in simulations or role-playing exercises to prepare for real-world decisions.

Adaptability is another core tenet of military decision-making. The concept of the OODA loop—Observe, Orient, Decide, Act—originated in the military and has since been adopted across various fields. This iterative process encourages leaders to continuously evaluate their environment, adapt their strategies accordingly, and respond with agility. In high-pressure scenarios, the ability to remain open to new information and adjust decisions based on evolving circumstances can be the difference between success and failure. The OODA loop exemplifies the need for a dynamic approach to decision-making, one that embraces change rather than resists it.

Understanding the strengths and weaknesses of one's team is critical. In the military, leaders rely on their teams, knowing that effective delegation and trust are paramount. This is particularly important in high-stakes decision-making, where collaboration and teamwork can enhance the quality of decisions and execution. Leaders who cultivate an environment of trust and foster open communication channels empower their teams to contribute valuable insights. Learning to leverage the diverse skills and perspectives within a team can significantly enhance the decision-making process.

Military leaders also know when to follow their instincts. While data and analysis are invaluable, there are moments when intuition plays a critical role. Military training and experience sharpen intuitive skills, teaching leaders when it's appropriate to rely on gut feelings. This balance between data-driven decision-making and intuitive judgment is essential. Leaders who can effectively integrate both approaches are often more adept at navigating complex and ambiguous situations.

Effective risk management is another lesson to be taken from the military approach to decision-making. Weighing risks and probabilities, while considering the potential impact of failure, is part of the decision-making toolkit. Military leaders often assess risk with sober realism, acknowledging both the potential for success and the dangers of failure. This pragmatic approach can be applied to business and other sectors, helping leaders to make informed decisions that balance opportunity with potential fallout.

Furthermore, after-action reviews, or AARs, are a staple of military operations, providing a structured way to reflect on decisions and learn from them. By analyzing what worked well and what didn't, leaders can gain invaluable insights that inform future decision-making. Implementing a similar practice in any professional setting can promote a culture of continuous improvement, encouraging leaders and their teams to learn from each experience, whether successful or not.

Empathy and ethical considerations also play a crucial role in military decisions. While mission objectives are important, considering the broader human and ethical implications of decisions ensures that actions align with core values. Leaders who prioritize empathy in decision-making often find that their choices resonate better with their teams and stakeholders, building trust and strengthening relationships.

Finally, resilience is at the heart of effective decision-making in the military. The ability to recover quickly from setbacks and maintain a strong, focused mindset is key to navigating high-pressure environments. Military training often emphasizes mental toughness and resilience, equipping leaders to handle stress and avoid paralysis in times of uncertainty. By fostering resilience, professionals can enhance their capacity to make sound decisions, even in the most challenging circumstances.

In summary, military approaches to high-stakes decisions provide a rich tapestry of techniques and mindsets from which professionals can learn. Strategic preparation, adaptability, experiential learning, and effective risk management form the cornerstone of military decision-making. When coupled with strong teamwork, intuitive judgment, and a commitment to continuous improvement, these approaches empower leaders to face high-pressure scenarios with confidence and clarity. By integrating these lessons, decision-makers can sharpen their skills and bolster their ability to navigate the challenges that lie ahead.

Chapter 6: Communication in High-Pressure Situations

Communication in high-pressure situations isn't just about conveying information; it's about creating understanding and fostering trust when the stakes are high. Whether you're in a boardroom facing a critical decision or on the frontlines of an unexpected crisis, the ability to relay your message clearly and listen intently influences the outcome. Effective communication starts with clarity—articulating your thoughts concisely and ensuring they resonate with your audience. But it's not only about speaking; it's equally critical to listen, tuning into verbal and non-verbal cues, as they provide insights into others' perspectives and emotions. By actively listening, you can adapt your approach based on feedback, which not only empowers your decision-making process but also strengthens collaboration and mutual respect. In essence, mastering communication amid pressure isn't about controlling the narrative; it's about nurturing a dialogue that guides the team towards informed and confident choices.

The Art of Clear Communication

In high-pressure situations, communication becomes the lifeline that connects ideas, decisions, and outcomes. The ability to convey thoughts and instructions clearly can be the difference between success and failure. It's not merely about speaking or writing; it's about ensuring that your message is understood exactly as you intended. In moments of intense pressure, clarity isn't just preferred — it's essential.

Consider the environment of a bustling emergency room or a rapidly evolving corporate board meeting. In these settings, clarity in communication isn't a luxury, it's a necessity. When stakes are high, the margin for error narrows. Miscommunications can lead to critical mistakes with far-reaching consequences. Thus, mastering clear communication becomes a critical skill for any professional seeking to navigate these tumultuous waters effectively.

At its core, clear communication is about simplicity and precision. This doesn't mean reducing complex ideas to sound bites or oversimplifying issues to the point of inaccuracy. Rather, it involves distilling complex information into accessible language that retains its essential nuances. It's about speaking to be understood, not just heard.

The Importance of Context

When communicating under pressure, context is king. Understanding the environmental and interpersonal dynamics at play is crucial. A message tailored to its context will resonate more deeply and be less prone to misinterpretation. Effective communicators probe the space around them, asking themselves how their message might be perceived and what additional information might be necessary for clarity. They recognize that what works in one scenario might fall flat in another.

Imagine you're tasked with delivering a crucial project update to stakeholders who're unfamiliar with its technical intricacies. Here, the art of communication lies in balancing detailed insights with broader, goal-oriented language. By anchoring technical details in the project's overarching objectives, you provide context which helps listeners connect the dots more effectively.

Listening as a Component of Communication

Too often, communication is misconceived as a one-way street. Yet, listening is just as crucial, especially in high-pressure environments. Active listening isn't passive; it involves engaging with the speaker, asking questions, and confirming understanding. It's how leaders gather essential information before making decisions and how they ensure their teams feel understood and valued.

In practice, this means taking a step back during discussions and truly absorbing what other parties are saying. It requires withholding judgment until all facts and viewpoints have been presented and recognized. This not only aids in making informed decisions but also fosters an environment of trust — a key component when pressure mounts.

Nonverbal Communication and Its Influence

Never underestimate the power of nonverbal cues. In high-pressure scenarios, your body language, facial expressions, and tone can communicate volumes, often providing more credibility than words alone. Effective communicators maintain awareness of these elements to bolster their messages. A confident posture, steady eye contact, and a composed tone can reinforce clarity, while unconscious cues can potentially undermine verbal messages.

Train yourself to observe both your own nonverbal signals and those of others. Are team members nodding in agreement, or do their expressions suggest confusion? These cues can guide you in adjusting your approach, ensuring that you're not just speaking, but truly communicating.

The Role of Empathy

Empathy is an overlooked yet essential component of clear communication, particularly under stress. Understanding the perspectives and emotional states of those you're communicating with can dramatically improve the effectiveness of your interactions. Empathy allows you to tailor messages so they resonate more deeply with your audience's needs and concerns.

In practice, this involves considering the personal and professional pressures others might be experiencing and taking these factors into account when crafting your message. Empathic communication is not only clear but also considerate, fostering stronger connections and a more cohesive team dynamic.

Practicing Clarity Under Pressure

Clarity is a skill honed through practice and reflection. In high-pressure situations, the natural human response is to react quickly — sometimes at the expense of clarity. Train yourself to pause, review your message, and consider its reception before communicating. This short moment of reflection can lead to more precise, purposeful communication.

Developing templates or communication frameworks for common scenarios can also be beneficial. These tools, built from experience, can serve as guides to ensure that your core messages remain consistent and clear, even when the pressure is on.

Conclusion

The art of clear communication is a cornerstone skill for those who navigate high-pressure environments. It's a discipline that integrates simplicity with depth, and empathy with assertiveness. By prioritizing clear communication, you enhance decision-making abilities, foster stronger teams, and ultimately drive more successful outcomes. In the fast-paced world we often find ourselves in, there's no greater tool at our disposal than the capacity to communicate with clarity and purpose.

Listening Effectively

In any high-pressure situation, effective listening is not just a skill—it's a cornerstone of successful communication. The chaotic demands of urgent decision-making environments often compel professionals to prioritize speaking and immediate responses over active listening. Yet, truly listening to others can transform interactions, leading to better outcomes and innovation. As we navigate the intricacies of communication under pressure, understanding how to listen effectively becomes a pivotal asset.

To start, what does it mean to listen effectively, particularly when the stakes are high? At its core, effective listening is about understanding, not just the words being spoken, but the emotions, intentions, and context behind them. This requires more than a passive receipt of information. It's an active engagement that demands focus, empathy, and a willingness to quiet our internal chatter. In these moments, being fully present allows us to absorb not only what's being said but also what remains unspoken.

An essential element of effective listening is empathy. Empathic listening involves genuinely putting oneself in another person's shoes, striving to understand their perspective without judgment. In high-pressure situations, where quick resolutions are often sought, taking the time to understand someone's viewpoint can unveil important insights that might otherwise be overlooked. It creates a space where individuals feel valued, fostering an environment that encourages open communication and collaboration.

Moreover, in high-stakes environments, the art of listening involves deciphering non-verbal cues. Often, body language, facial expressions, and tone of voice convey more than words. Being attuned to these signals enhances our understanding of the message being delivered, providing a richer context and deeper insight. By honing this skill, you're likely to catch nuances that would otherwise be missed, leading to more informed and considered decisions.

However, barriers to effective listening are abundant, especially in pressured settings. Stress and adrenaline can cloud judgment and sharpen the impulse to respond immediately, rather than taking a moment to truly listen. Our own biases and preconceptions act as filters that distort the information we receive. Overcoming these barriers requires not just awareness but active suppression of the instinct to react prematurely. It's about suspending judgment, consciously setting aside distractions, and practicing patience even when the pressure mounts most intensely.

Active listening techniques can significantly aid our ability to listen effectively. Paraphrasing, or summarizing back what the speaker has shared, is a powerful tool that ensures not only comprehension but also validates the speaker's message. This technique reassures others that their input is valued, reinforcing their contribution to the discourse. Similarly, asking open-ended questions can promote further dialogue and uncover layers of information critical to comprehensive understanding.

In high-pressure situations, leaders often set the tone for communication dynamics. By exemplifying effective listening, they not only gather vital information but also cultivate a culture of trust and respect. This culture can permeate through teams, encouraging others to adopt similar practices. As more individuals commit to truly understanding their colleagues, the synergy and cohesiveness of the team strengthen, driving more effective and harmonious decision-making.

Of course, listening is a two-way street. While focusing on understanding others, it is equally important to ensure one's own message is being accurately conveyed and received. Clarity and consistency are vital when communicating in high-stakes scenarios, ensuring there is no room for misinterpretation. Effective listeners also seek feedback on their own communication styles, refining them to remove potential obstacles to understanding.

For professionals seeking to improve their listening abilities, practice remains key. This practice could involve deliberate and focused listening sessions, where attention is entirely devoted to understanding the other person without interjection. Over time, this "listening muscle" becomes stronger and more intuitive, integrating into everyday interactions and shining bright during moments of significant pressure.

Listening effectively is more than just a communication skill; it's a decision-making strategy that empowers professionals to engage confidently in their environments. By listening actively and empathetically, you unlock the potential for deeper connections and informed decisions. This will not only enhance your performance in high-pressure scenarios but also enrich your interpersonal relationships, driving better outcomes both professionally and personally.

In conclusion, by committing to listen effectively, professionals can transform their decision-making processes. As you hone this ability, you contribute to an organizational culture that values understanding and collaboration. The investment in developing this skill pays dividends in the form of more informed decisions and stronger relationships, ultimately leading to an environment where both individuals and teams thrive under the pressures that come their way.

Chapter 7: Time Management and Prioritization Strategies

Navigating high-pressure environments requires not only quick thinking but also a mastery of time management and prioritization. Integrating these skills into your decision-making toolkit can make all the difference when the stakes are high. The ability to sift through mountains of tasks and pinpoint what truly matters is crucial. It's about identifying the intersection of urgency and importance, which demands both intuition and structured planning. Time is your most finite resource, and how you allocate it reflects directly on the outcomes you achieve. By sharpening your focus on strategic priorities, you empower yourself to make not just rapid decisions, but smart ones, ensuring that pressure doesn't impede your progress. When every second counts, clarity of purpose and a disciplined approach to prioritization can transform challenges into opportunities, driving sustainable success even in the most frenetic situations.

Techniques for Rapid Decision-Making

In the ever-evolving landscape of professional life, the ability to make swift and confident decisions can distinguish the success stories from the cautionary tales. It's not just about moving fast but about making the right moves swiftly. Techniques for rapid decision-making are vital in environments where each moment counts, and hesitation can lead to missed opportunities or increased risks. While the stakes might vary from one decision to another, the strategies to tackle them effectively remain consistent, empowering you to act with purpose and precision.

First and foremost, clarity of purpose is paramount. Knowing what you aim to achieve sets the groundwork for making fast decisions. This involves a thorough understanding of your objectives, which aligns with your broader strategic goals. Clarity narrows down choices, thus speeding up the decision-making process. When time is of the essence, this elimination of unnecessary options is a time-saver.

Next up is the mastery of prioritization. Not every decision demands the same level of urgency or critical analysis. This is where distinguishing between urgency and importance comes into play. It's crucial to develop the habit of categorizing tasks based on their impact and deadline. Rapid decision-makers often employ mental or physical matrices to visualize where specific tasks and decisions fall. By systematically prioritizing, you can focus your cognitive resources on what truly matters in critical moments.

Another powerful technique is honing intuition through continuous learning and experience accumulation. Over time, familiarity with similar scenarios develops a gut feeling or an instinctive response that can guide rapid decisions. This is an intuitive leap based on patterns recognized subconsciously, built from years of observation and analysis. While intuition shouldn't replace data-driven decisions, it is invaluable when you need to act quickly with limited information.

Embracing a decision-making framework can also streamline your process. A systematic approach tailored to your personal or organizational needs ensures consistency and confidence in the decisions made. Whether it's the OODA loop (Observe, Orient, Decide, Act), the RAPID framework (Recommend, Agree, Perform, Input, Decide), or another model, having a structure helps reduce the cognitive load, allowing for quicker, more effective decisions.

Moreover, seeking diverse perspectives swiftly is a technique often underrated. When decisions are required at a breakneck speed, drawing on the expertise and insights of diverse team members can illuminate blind spots and provide a more rounded view. Rapid information-gathering from trusted advisors or team members can lead to more informed decisions while avoiding analysis paralysis.

In tandem with gathering insights is the principle of making a decision with the available information. Waiting for perfect information can lead to delays and, ultimately, lost opportunities. It is important to accept the inherent uncertainty of decision-making and take action with the best information at hand. This aligns with the '80/20 rule'—identifying that in many cases, 80% of consequences come from 20% of causes, suggesting that getting to 80% certainty can often be sufficient for confident decisions.

Furthermore, rapid decision-making benefits from emotional intelligence. Stress and high-pressure environments can cloud judgment. Practicing emotional regulation techniques, from mindfulness to quick stress-relief strategies, can maintain clarity and focus. When you keep emotions in check and create a calm mental space, you're better positioned to make objective and efficient decisions, even in stressful situations.

Feedback loops also play an integral role in rapid decision-making. Establishing a system for feedback allows you to evaluate the outcomes of your quick decisions. This feedback not only guides future choices but also builds confidence in your decision-making agility. Learning from past outcomes can refine your process, ensuring more accuracy and efficiency the next time you're faced with a similar situation.

Finally, technology can be a pivotal ally in enhancing decision speed. From AI-driven analytics to decision-support tools, leveraging technology can speed up the analysis process, providing data-driven insights at a fraction of the time. Familiarizing yourself with these tools can give you a competitive edge, ensuring you stay a step ahead.

In conclusion, rapid decision-making isn't about rushing; it's about making informed choices swiftly and efficiently. As you develop these techniques, you'll discover that quick decisions often result from a well-oiled strategy machine rather than spontaneous action. With clarity, prioritization, intuition, frameworks, diverse input, emotional intelligence, feedback, and technology, you can craft a robust approach that not only saves time but also enhances decision quality. High-stakes environments demand no less.

Balancing Urgency with Importance

In the fast-paced realm of high-stakes decisions, professionals often grapple with the challenge of balancing urgency with importance. It's a critical aspect of time management and prioritization that can dictate success or failure. The sense of urgency often comes with a palpable need to act swiftly, while importance demands a strategic focus on long-term goals. Mastering this balance equips decision-makers with the clarity and confidence to tackle even the most daunting challenges.

At the heart of balancing urgency and importance lies the *Eisenhower Matrix*, a tool that continues to serve leaders by categorizing tasks based on their urgency and importance. Tasks falling into the quadrant of high importance and high urgency rightfully demand immediate attention. However, many professionals mistakenly focus on what seems urgent rather than what's truly important, often leading to burnout and inefficiency. Striving for balance requires reflection and a keen awareness of one's goals and values.

Emotional intelligence plays a crucial role. When stakes are high, emotions can cloud judgment, leading individuals to misjudge the urgency or overlook significant factors. The ability to regulate emotions and maintain composure allows for better assessment of what demands immediate action and what can be thoughtfully planned. This combination of emotional awareness and importance-oriented thinking keeps professionals aligned with their core mission, steering clear of distractions.

Consideration of impact is another essential piece of the puzzle. High-impact tasks, even if not seemingly urgent, contribute significantly to long-term objectives. Strategic leaders prioritize these tasks by clearly outlining their potential benefits and aligning them with broader organizational goals. On the other hand, tasks that are both urgent and of low importance might be skillfully delegated or automated, allowing decision-makers to focus their energy where it truly counts.

Moreover, effective delegation emerges as a powerful strategy in balancing urgent and important tasks. By empowering team members, leaders can ensure urgent tasks are handled with the required immediacy without diverting focus from the important work. Delegation not only alleviates individual pressure but also cultivates a learning environment where teams grow through shared responsibility. This creates a ripple effect of capability across the organization.

Reflection periods are an often-overlooked yet vital aspect of managing urgency and importance. By scheduling regular moments of reflection, decision-makers can reassess priorities, identify patterns in their urgency-importance balance, and refine their strategies. Reflection also helps in recognizing the signs of "urgency addiction," a tendency to feel overly compelled to address urgent tasks at the expense of important ones. Being mindful of this pitfall helps maintain an appropriate focus.

Effective time management often requires saying "no" to tasks that do not serve long-term goals. Professionals need to cultivate the courage to protect their schedules against low-impact urgencies masquerading as priorities. By doing so, they not only enhance their decision-making capacity but also inspire their teams to adopt a similar disciplined approach, reinforcing a culture focused on value over immediacy.

Ultimately, striking the right balance between urgency and importance is a dynamic process. It requires constant adaptation as circumstances evolve, necessitating flexibility without compromising on strategic objectives. Leaders must be proactive rather than reactive, seizing the moment to address what's paramount while remaining agile to shift focus as new information and challenges arise.

Learning from past experiences further enhances one's ability to discern urgency and importance. Historical data and reflective insights serve as vital tools, enabling decision-makers to predict potential urgencies and prepare for them without sacrificing important long-term goals. By leveraging historical patterns, they can anticipate outcomes and make informed choices that harmonize immediate needs with future aspirations.

Ultimately, balancing urgency with importance is more than just a skill; it's a mindset. It calls for discipline, foresight, and empathy, not only within oneself but towards one's team. This mindset fosters a supportive environment where critical decisions are made with both precision and vision, advancing individual and organizational growth. In high-pressure arenas, this balance becomes the cornerstone that distinguishes exceptional leaders from the rest.

Chapter 8: Stress Management for Better Decision-Making

In the demanding world of high-stakes decisions, managing stress effectively becomes a cornerstone for clearer thinking and improved choices. When pressure mounts, it can cloud judgment, making even the simplest decisions feel daunting. By embracing stress management techniques, professionals not only maintain composure but also enhance their decision-making prowess. Start by fostering mindfulness to anchor your thoughts, allowing you to remain present amidst chaos. Practicing regular physical activity and engaging in deep breathing exercises can significantly reduce stress levels, providing a clearer headspace. Building resilience through adaptable thinking and nurturing a positive outlook turns stress into a manageable element rather than an overwhelming force. Remember, stress, when handled well, can be a motivator rather than a barrier, sharpening your ability to make confident and informed decisions under pressure. In doing so, you transform potential stress into a powerful tool that aids rather than hinders your journey in high-pressure environments.

Techniques to Stay Calm Under Pressure

In the heat of the moment, when decisions swarm you like buzzing bees, staying calm can feel like an elusive ideal. Yet, it's within the calm that clarity resides—a crucial asset for anyone tasked with making high-stakes decisions. We often hear that pressure is part and parcel of decision-making, but the key lies not in avoiding pressure, but in harnessing it. This section aims to arm you with effective techniques to maintain your composure and allow the best version of you to step forward when it matters most.

The first technique to mastering calm is deep breathing. Although it may sound overly simplistic, deep breathing is scientifically proven to reduce stress and increase focus. When you breathe deeply, you signal your body to relax, thus entering a state where logical thinking can dominate over emotional responses. Practice inhaling through your nose for four counts, holding for four, and then exhaling through your mouth for another four counts. This rhythmic breathing brings you back to the present moment, providing the mental space needed to evaluate your options.

Mindfulness is another valuable tool in your arsenal to tackle pressure. Mindfulness involves honing your focus on the here and now, even when everything around you screams for attention. By training yourself to be present, you reduce the influence of external stressors. Set aside a few minutes each day to practice mindfulness meditation; this can range from sitting quietly to noticing the sensations in your body or simply acknowledging your thoughts without judgment. This daily practice strengthens your ability to remain centered during high-pressure situations, turning what could be chaotic moments into opportunities for thoughtful reflection.

An often-overlooked technique for staying calm under pressure is preparation. When you're well-prepared, you inherently feel more confident and less anxious about the outcomes. Anticipate potential scenarios and rehearse your responses. Making use of mental simulations can effectively prepare you for what's to come. Think of it as setting a mental map; having landmarks in mind reduces anxiety and fosters a sense of control, hence bolstering calmness when pressure strikes.

Next, let's talk about setting priorities—managing what's truly important. Pressure often arises from the sheer volume of decisions that demand immediate attention. Decision fatigue sets in, making each subsequent choice more complex. By prioritizing tasks, you allocate your energy and focus wisely. Apply tools such as the Eisenhower Box to discern between what's urgent and important. Executing this strategy ensures you're not overwhelmed, which facilitates a calm demeanor when targeted decisions need making.

Visualization also plays a powerful role in maintaining calm under pressure. Before a high-stakes situation, visualize yourself navigating through the pressure adeptly and achieving a positive outcome. This technique programs your subconscious mind to act as if you have already succeeded, enhancing your confidence and your ability to remain calm. Imagine the environment, the people, the challenges, and visualize yourself dealing with them effectively. This mental rehearsal can demystify nerve-racking situations, reducing their perceived complexity, and increasing your composure.

Reframing negative thoughts boosts your resilience under pressure. It's easy to spiral into a cycle of pessimism when stressed, but by actively reframing your thoughts, you can alter your response to stress. Instead of seeing a high-pressure situation as a threat, view it as an opportunity to showcase your problem-solving skills. Affirm positive outcomes and remind yourself of past successes where you thrived under similar conditions. This mental shift fosters a growth mindset that views challenges as learning experiences.

Another vital component is adequate **sleep and rest**. It might seem trivial amidst a busy schedule, but compromise on sleep can lead to impaired judgment and heightened stress. Ensure that rest becomes an integral part of your routine. Whether through a good night's sleep or short breaks throughout the day, these moments of rest reset your stress levels, refresh your mind, and strengthen your ability to handle pressure with calm assurance.

Don't underestimate the power of reaching out to your support system. When the pressure mounts, having someone to confide in can alleviate stress. Conversations with trusted colleagues or mentors offer fresh perspectives and solutions that you might not have considered. They can help dissect overwhelming situations into manageable parts, turning anxiety into achievable action plans. Cultivating these relationships provides a buffer against the isolation often felt in high-pressure scenarios, reminding you that collaboration is possible even in times of stress.

Incorporating regular exercise into your routine is another valuable technique to maintain calm under pressure. Physical activity releases endorphins—natural mood lifters—that equip your body to handle stress better. Whether it's a brisk walk, a cycling session, or any form of exercise, these activities mitigate anxiety levels while improving cognitive functions. The discipline and focus required in staying physically active transit into mental clarity and emotional regulation during challenging decision-making moments.

Finally, practice gratitude. It might seem counterintuitive to think about being grateful when you're under pressure, but this simple act can ground you and shift focus away from anxiety. Reflect on what is positive in your life and within the situation at hand. Gratitude changes your perspective, spotlighting the good amidst the stressful, thus relaxing the tight grip of pressure on your psyche.

Each of these techniques, from breathing and mindfulness to preparation and gratitude, lays the foundation for a robust approach to stress management. By integrating these practices into your daily routine, you sharpen your decision-making tools, ready to face high-pressure scenarios with poise. Remember, the goal is not to eliminate pressure but to transform it into a stepping stone for decisive success.

Building Resilience

In the world of high-stakes decision-making, resilience isn't just a trait—it's a necessity. It's the backbone that supports you when pressure mounts and clarity seems miles away. Building resilience means more than just bouncing back from setbacks; it involves developing the capacity to adapt, learn, and thrive despite adversity. This section aims to provide insights and techniques to bolster your resilience, enhancing your capability to make sound decisions under stress.

Resilience in decision-making begins with acknowledging that setbacks are not failures but opportunities to gain insights and grow stronger. The way you perceive challenges significantly influences how resilient you'll be in handling them. Developing a growth mindset, one where you view obstacles as stepping stones rather than roadblocks, is crucial. This mindset shift aligns with the concept of stress-related growth, where enduring difficulties fosters an increase in personal strength and wisdom.

One practical approach to building resilience is through cultivating emotional regulation. Often, high-pressure situations trigger intense emotions that can cloud judgment. Techniques such as mindfulness and meditation have proven effective in enhancing emotional regulation. By training your mind to focus and remain calm, you allow yourself the mental space needed to evaluate options objectively and make clearer decisions.

Furthermore, self-awareness plays a pivotal role in resilience. Understanding your stress triggers and knowing how you typically respond to pressure can help you prepare and develop strategies to manage these reactions better. Self-reflection through journaling is a beneficial way to increase this awareness. It involves taking a step back to analyze your experiences and feelings, which can reveal patterns in your decision-making process.

Another cornerstone of resilience is developing a supportive network. Decisions made in isolation can amplify stress and pressure. By building a community of trusted colleagues, mentors, or networks, you create a safety net for bouncing ideas, sharing burdens, and gaining new perspectives. Collaborative resilience, where teams support each other, can transform the way organizations make decisions collectively.

Physical well-being also underpins your capacity to remain resilient in the face of stress. Regular exercise, a balanced diet, and sufficient rest are foundational elements that shouldn't be overlooked. Physical health directly affects mental clarity and stamina, equipping you to face challenges head-on. Incorporating physical activities that you enjoy into your routine can help mitigate stress and foster a habit of resilience.

Moreover, setting realistic goals and managing expectations is an often underrated aspect of resilience. When goals are set too high without consideration for potential obstacles, the risk of burnout increases. Instead, approaching tasks with a mindset that accepts imperfection can enhance resilience by reducing self-imposed pressure and emphasizing progress over perfection.

It's also essential to cultivate flexibility and adaptability. The landscape of decision-making is ever-changing, and clinging to rigid plans can hinder resilience. Embracing adaptability means being open to new ideas and willing to adjust courses of action as new information arises. It requires a balance between maintaining focus on your objectives while also being receptive to change.

Learning from past decisions, whether deemed successes or failures, fortifies resilience. Consider conducting decision reviews where you examine choices, understanding what worked, and identifying areas for improvement. This practice not only strengthens personal resilience but encourages a culture of continuous learning and refinement of decision-making strategies among your team or organization.

Finally, building resilience necessitates the cultivation of optimism. Viewing the future with a positive outlook doesn't remove challenges, but it equips you with a belief in your ability to navigate through them. Optimism fuels perseverance, turning setbacks into setups for future opportunities. Balancing optimism with realism ensures you remain hopeful without losing touch with reality.

Ultimately, resilience is about building internal and external resources that enable you to weather the storms of decision-making. It's a dynamic skill that continually evolves as you face new challenges and learn from them. By strengthening your resilience, you not only improve your decision-making capabilities but also enhance your ability to lead confidently in high-pressure situations.

Chapter 9: The Role of Data in Decision-Making

In the fast-paced world of high-stakes decision-making, data stands as a formidable ally, providing clarity amidst uncertainty. When time is short and the stakes are high, embracing data-driven insights can transform ambiguity into actionable knowledge. Analytics allow professionals to discern patterns, predict outcomes, and weigh potential risks against rewards with confidence. Yet, it's crucial not to be dazzled by numbers alone. Recognizing the limitations of data—such as potential biases and incomplete datasets—is essential in avoiding misleading conclusions. By marrying robust analytical skills with critical thinking, decision-makers can harness data strategically, sidestepping the pitfall of analysis paralysis while ensuring they remain attuned to the broader context. This balance empowers them to execute informed choices that drive success, even under pressure.

Leveraging Analytics for Informed Choices

In the realm of decision-making, data isn't just a supporting actor; it's a pivotal force that shapes the best outcomes. Analytics offers a powerful method to discern patterns, predict trends, and, crucially, reduce uncertainty in high-stakes environments. For professionals entrenched in decision-intensive roles, leveraging analytics doesn't merely aid decisions—it transforms them.

Let's consider a scenario. You're a leader in a dynamic industry where stakes are high and the margins for error are razor-thin. Strategic choices here can lead to exponential growth or catastrophic loss. Analytics enables you to shift from instinct-driven to evidence-driven decision-making. It's akin to navigating a fog-laden ocean with a lighthouse to guide you safely to shore. The decisions once shrouded in ambiguity become clearer as patterns emerge through the effective use of data.

The core value of analytics in decision-making lies in its precision. By quantitatively evaluating variables, professionals can mitigate biases and assumptions that could potentially skew judgment. Cognitive biases—like overconfidence or the anchoring effect—often cloud our decision-making process without us even realizing it. When data takes center stage, it becomes a balance to those biases, facilitating decisions that rest not on gut feel but on hard evidence.

However, the value extracted from data hinges on the quality of the analytics used. Raw data, as massive as it may be, holds no inherent wisdom or judgment. It is the meticulous process of analysis that elevates it from mere numbers on a spreadsheet to actionable insights that can drive organizational success. Advanced analytical tools and models enable professionals to dissect data sets to unearth correlations and causal relationships that might not be immediately apparent. For example, predictive analytics can identify emerging market trends, allowing companies to anticipate customer needs even before they express them directly.

It's important to address the misconception that analytics only serves quantitative fields. In reality, qualitative insights are equally valuable. Text analytics, for instance, can help shed light on customer sentiment by sifting through massive amounts of unstructured text, such as reviews or surveys. The synthesis of both quantitative and qualitative analytics provides a comprehensive view of the landscape, supporting diverse decision-making paradigms across industries.

Effective use of analytics can also empower professionals to construct dynamic models that simulate different scenarios. This approach provides a sandbox for testing how different variables will play out in practice before committing to a course of action in reality. Not only does this reduce risk, but it also instills a degree of confidence in actions taken because the outcomes have been deemed probable through rigorous testing.

Yet, with the power of analytics comes the responsibility to ask the right questions. The most sophisticated analytical tools will falter if directed by the wrong inquiries. Decision-makers are tasked with defining the scope and boundaries of the analysis: What problem needs solving? Which variables hold significance? Moreover, they must be mindful of context. Data doesn't exist in a vacuum; rather, it often interacts and coexists with other variables, and understanding this interplay is crucial to making informed decisions.

Adopting data-driven decision-making involves a cultural shift within organizations. Leaders must not only embrace the tools and methodologies but also foster an atmosphere where data-informed decisions are valued and encouraged. Training and skill development play a vital role in this transition. It's not enough to have access to cutting-edge technology—understanding how to extract value from it is equally critical.

For example, many organizations have integrated data literacy programs, ensuring that all team members—from executives to junior staff—are proficient in basic data analysis and interpretation. Such initiatives democratize the use of data within an organization, breaking the silo of information and making analytics a shared asset.

While embracing analytics, professionals must also confront inherent limitations. Not all data is created equal, and erroneous data can steer decisions astray. Data quality and integrity are paramount. Moreover, even with pristine data, predictions aren't certainties. Unpredictable factors can always alter predicted outcomes, making it essential to maintain flexibility and adaptability.

This leads us to the concept of continuous improvement. As the data landscape evolves, so should the strategies for collecting, managing, and analyzing that data. Professionals must commit to ever-evolving analytical methods and stay abreast of technological advancements. This rigorous pursuit of improvement allows organizations to continually refine their decision-making processes, ensuring they remain competitive and are better equipped to handle the challenges of tomorrow.

It's worth emphasizing how analytics helps in realizing the potential of collective intelligence. By using data to validate or challenge opinions, diverse teams can converge on a more informed collective decision. This process can help resolve conflicts, minimize individual biases, and harness the group's wisdom effectively.

Finally, remember that while analytics provides a formidable edge, it's the human touch— the intuition, creativity, and experience of the decision-maker—that ultimately turns data into action. This synergy between man and machine, if well-managed, can unlock new heights in the art of decision-making.

In conclusion, leveraging analytics for informed choices transforms challenges into opportunities, enabling professionals to confidently navigate the complexities of high-pressure environments, informed by comprehensive, data-driven insights. It equips them with the vision to not only recognize immediate ripples but also anticipate future waves, making the analyst a modern oracle in an ever-changing world.

Understanding Data Limitations

In today's fast-paced, data-driven world, we often find ourselves surrounded by numbers, charts, and statistics. Data can guide decisions, inform strategies, and offer insights that weren't possible a decade ago. But with this abundance comes a critical need to understand the limitations of data, especially when making high-stakes decisions. This understanding isn't about diminishing the role of data; instead, it's about recognizing where data meets its boundaries and where human judgment becomes paramount.

Imagine relying solely on data without considering its context. Numbers can tell you what happened but may not always be able to explain why it happened or what will happen next. For professionals under pressure, the distinction between causal relationships and mere correlations can mean the difference between a decision that moves the organization forward and one that leads to unforeseen complications. Take, for instance, the error of mistaking correlation for causation. While data might show a positive trend in sales whenever a particular advertisement runs, it doesn't inherently prove the ad was the sole driver of increased sales.

Moreover, data is never free from the influence of biases. We often encounter the danger of confirmation bias—interpreting data in a way that confirms our preconceived notions while ignoring evidence to the contrary. This can lead to decision-making that feels safe and comfortable but might not be grounded in reality. As decision-makers, cultivating an awareness of our biases and actively seeking opposing data can help us see the bigger picture and make more balanced choices.

Then there is the issue of data quality. No dataset is immune to errors. Incomplete data, outdated information, or inaccurate entries can significantly skew the results. For example, if you're basing a decision on customer feedback but only have data from a non-representative sample, your conclusion might not reflect the true opinion of your broader customer base. This makes it crucial to question the reliability of data sources and, where possible, to triangulate findings using multiple data points.

Considering the rapidly changing environment in which we operate, relevance becomes a major factor. Data that was relevant a month ago might no longer hold the same value today. In volatile markets, today's breakthrough can swiftly become tomorrow's outdated strategy. Decision-makers must continually refresh their data insights, ensuring that they are acting on the most current information available. Failing to do so could lead to choices that are based on historical circumstances that no longer exist.

In understanding data limitations, it's also vital to grasp the concept of data representation and visualization. How data is presented can greatly influence our perception. A well-constructed graph can convey an accurate story, while a misleading one can skew interpretation, leading decision-makers down the wrong path. Thus, learning to critically evaluate data presentations is an essential skill for minimizing misinterpretation risks.

The quantitative nature of data can sometimes overshadow qualitative insights that are equally crucial. Numbers can tell you "how much" but often fail to explain "how" or "why" in human terms. This limitation points to the need for combining quantitative data with qualitative insights. Stories, feedback, and human experiences can provide context, fill gaps, and offer depth that purely numerical data might overlook.

It's worth noting that data is most valuable when it guides decisions rather than dictates them. Structured frameworks can help in systematically evaluating how data aligns with overarching goals and principles. By doing so, we can navigate complexity with figures while maintaining alignment with our core values and objectives.

Another pressing challenge is the overwhelming volume of data, often referred to as "information overload." It can be paralyzing, leading to analysis paralysis—overanalyzing information to the point where a decision is never made. Here, prioritization strategies become crucial, helping decision-makers cut through the noise and focus on data that truly matters.

In conclusion, data is a powerful tool, but recognizing its limitations is crucial for anyone aiming to make informed and effective decisions under pressure. Knowing when to trust data and when to listen to intuitive judgment is an art that comes with practice, awareness, and the ability to embrace uncertainty. By maintaining a critical eye and a flexible mindset, decision-makers can navigate the complex interplay of data and intuition, crafting strategies that are both analytically sound and humanly wise.

Chapter 10: Trusting Intuition in Decision-Making

In the realm of high-stakes decision-making, intuition isn't just a whimsical hunch; it's a critical tool aligned by years of experience and deep-seated knowledge. While the analytical mind meticulously sifts through data, it's sometimes the spark of intuition that catalyzes the final decision, connecting the dots in a way logic alone may not. Professionals in demanding environments might hesitate to trust their gut, fearing it lacks the rigor of empirical evidence. However, intuition isn't detached from facts; it's often a culmination of subconscious insights drawn from patterns recognized over time. The key is knowing when to let intuition lead, particularly when decisions need to be made quickly and decisively. It's about harmonizing intuitive judgment with objective data, finding a balance that allows you to act with both confidence and acuity. Empowering yourself to trust your instincts while staying grounded in reality is a skill worth cultivating, transforming uncertainty into opportunity.

When to Rely on Gut Feelings

In the fast-paced world of high-stakes decision-making, where every choice can lead to significant outcomes, knowing when to rely on gut feelings isn't just beneficial—it's crucial. Intuition, that innate sense telling us which path to follow, often emerges from years of experience and amassed knowledge. Yet, amidst the pressure and high expectations, professionals frequently find themselves torn between intuition and rational analysis. The key lies in recognizing the situations where intuition can serve as a guide, providing a swift and effective pathway through complexity.

Let's break it down by understanding the mechanics of intuition. It's comparable to a highly sophisticated pattern recognition system, trained through innumerable disruptions and achievements (or failures). For instance, a veteran firefighter may enter a burning building and instinctively sense the structure's instability. These snap judgements aren't random; they're grounded in extensive experience. Therefore, to rely on gut feelings means having confidence in your wealth of personal insights, something that must be meticulously cultivated over time.

Despite its potential, people often undervalue intuition in decision-making, especially in corporate environments where data reigns supreme. Numbers and analytics seem to offer an objective standpoint, reducing perceived risks. However, while data provides clarity, it doesn't always capture the nuances of a situation. High-stakes decisions frequently involve unpredictable human elements and emotional nuances that data cannot quantify. Here, gut feelings can bridge the gap, filling the void with personal insight and tacit understanding.

One illustrative example might be choosing a business partner. Sure, you have spreadsheets, financial projections, and market analyses, but there's also the intangible factor of character and compatibility. Time and again, executives have shared stories where numbers said "yes," but their gut feelings warned against it. In retrospect, these ignored intuitive warnings often pointed out overlooked red flags.

When should intuition take the lead, then? It often shines when time is of the essence. High-pressure situations rarely afford the luxury of thorough analysis. In such instances, seasoned professionals recognize the power of intuition as a rapid decision-making tool. For instance, during an unexpected crisis, a leader might not have the luxury of delving into detailed data. Instead, their seasoned gut instincts guide their decisions swiftly and effectively, like a pilot navigating a sudden storm.

Recognizing familiarity in decision patterns can also signal when to trust your gut. If a situation closely resembles past experiences where outcomes were satisfactory, those prior successes can guide your current decision. The confidence derived from past successes, embodied in your gut feeling, can illuminate the path forward, minimizing hesitation.

Interestingly, intuition also manifests during collaborative efforts, where group dynamics come into play. Leaders often need quick insight into team morale or synergy. Here, gut feelings can help decode non-verbal cues or sense unspoken concerns, guiding leaders on how to foster trust or address potential friction before it becomes detrimental.

That being said, relying solely on gut feelings without any checks can be dangerous. Our instincts are not immune to cognitive biases. They can sometimes be clouded by personal prejudices, selective perceptions, or overconfidence in our abilities. Thus, a balance needs to be struck. Coupling instinctual decisions with critical reasoning, or using analytical tools as a supplement, can enhance the decision-making process and mitigate potential biases.

To harness the full potential of intuition, it's crucial to nurture it actively. This involves engaging in self-reflection and seeking feedback from peers—both avenues to challenge and refine your instinctual judgments. Encourage dialogue with mentors or colleagues about similar decisions and outcomes; their experiences might provide additional layers to your understanding. Over time, these practices sharpen your instinctual abilities, making gut intuition a more reliable ally.

Furthermore, professionals should foster environments where intuitive decision-making is valued, not shunned. Promote a culture that respects experiential knowledge alongside analytical skills. Team-building exercises and retreats can rejuvenate instinctive insights, encouraging risk-taking and learning, leading to greater acceptance of gut-led decisions.

Ultimately, the goal is to blend intuition with empirical evidence, not replace one with the other. When intuition aligns with data, it yields the most compelling decisions—trusting that tightrope between instinct and analysis. By knowing when and how to rely on gut feelings, you empower yourself to navigate through the fog of uncertainty with greater clarity and confidence.

In conclusion, decision-makers in high-pressure environments must master the art of balancing intuition with analytical thinking. Gut feelings serve as an immediate compass, directing us when reason alone may falter. By practicing and valuing this intrinsic guidance, professionals can make more informed, confident, and impactful decisions, even under the most pressing circumstances.

Combining Intuition with Facts

In the high-pressure world of decision-making, intuition often takes center stage, but it's crucial to remember that intuition should not act alone. It needs to be harmoniously balanced with factual data to yield the best outcomes. Intuition, as powerful and insightful as it can be, is not infallible. When combined with solid facts, it acts more as a comprehensive guide, leading us to enlightened decisions under even the most intense of circumstances.

Picture intuition as the seasoned sailor who can tell the storm is approaching just by the feel of the air and the sway of the ship. Facts are the precise instruments, the compass and the radar, that quantify the storm's path and intensity. Together, they ensure the ship navigates the storm with precision and insight. Just like a skilled sailor wouldn't rely solely on their gut feelings when venturing into treacherous waters, professionals shouldn't depend entirely on intuition without considering empirical evidence.

For professionals, the nature of high-stakes decisions often demands swift responses. In these moments, intuition serves as a rapid, subconscious assessment tool. It filters through years of experience, recognizing patterns we might not immediately see. However, intuition is also susceptible to biases, emotions, and incomplete information. This is where data and facts become invaluable. They ground intuition, providing a critical counterbalance to ensure decisions aren't swayed by subconscious biases or fleeting emotions that can cloud judgement.

Let's take a moment to consider the relationship between intuition and facts in terms of a concerto—a maestro and an orchestra. The maestro (our intuition) provides the interpretive vision, bringing music to life with passion and flair. Still, it's the orchestra (facts), with each note precise and well rehearsed, that delivers the full-bodied sound essential to the performance. Both intuition and facts have vital roles to play, but it's their synergy that brings harmony to decision-making.

The process of blending intuition with facts begins with gathering all relevant data. This step might feel cumbersome in time-sensitive scenarios, but it's an investment against possible misjudgments. Once the data is collected, the next step involves analysis. Here, intuition helps pinpoint which aspects demand focus by drawing parallels to previous experiences. Professionals often have extensive experience in their fields, and this experiential intuition can guide the interpretation of data with a level of personal insight that raw analysis alone might not provide.

Critical thinking plays a pivotal role in this balancing act. It involves questioning assumptions, investigating inconsistencies, and ensuring that reliance on intuition is supported with facts wherever possible. This brings us to an interesting intersection of the science and art of decision-making. Facts supply the scientific backbone, but intuition adds the artistic prowess, coloring decisions with foresight and creativity.

Effective decision-makers also understand the importance of circumstances. In some cases, the data can be overwhelming or ambiguous. In such situations, relying more heavily on intuition might be necessary. Conversely, when dealing with unfamiliar territories or novel situations, facts must take precedence while intuition adapts to new patterns. Decision-makers continually learn to adjust the weight they place on intuition and facts based on the context, demonstrating an intricate dance of flexibility and judgement.

Moreover, communication adds nuance to the integration process. Leaders who articulate the reasoning behind their decisions, leveraging both data and intuition, cultivate trust and transparency. By communicating how intuition aligns with the facts, they not only validate their own conclusions but also engage their teams, drawing on collective wisdom. When intuition and facts are presented together, they can overcome skepticism and foster a shared understanding amid complex decision-making environments.

For instance, business leaders frequently face decisions that have far-reaching consequences. Imagine a scenario where a company needs to decide on a strategic pivot. While data might indicate market trends and consumer behaviors, intuition offers insights into brand identity and cultural fit that numbers can't quantify. By anchoring intuitive insights in empirical evidence, leaders can create robust strategies that account for both quantitative and qualitative factors.

The courage to trust one's instincts should not lead to the discounting of data. Nor should the reliance on facts stifle the intuitive flow. The key is in equilibrium—knowing when to draw more upon intuition and when to lean on data-supported analysis. This balance is a powerful enabler, allowing professionals to move forward with confidence and clarity, even amid uncertainty.

In practical terms, developing this balance involves continuous refinement and reflection. Professionals should make a habit of recalling prior decisions, analyzing the roles intuition and facts played in those processes, and extrapolating lessons for the future. This reflective practice not only strengthens decision-making skills but also cultivates an instinctive understanding of how intuition and facts can best complement each other.

To sum up, the nexus of intuition and facts is not just a meeting point but a confluence that fuels effective decision-making. By deliberately interweaving instinctual insights with data-backed facts, professionals can enhance their ability to make nuanced and timely decisions, propelling their effectiveness to new heights in any high-stakes scenario. This harmony of intuition and facts becomes the guiding light, confidently leading the way through the uncertainties that invariably surface in the world of high-pressure decision-making.

Chapter 11: Ethical Considerations in High-Stakes Decisions

As professionals stand at the crossroads of high-stakes decisions, the ethical considerations inherent in these moments can't be ignored. It's vital to navigate moral dilemmas with a compass grounded in core values, ensuring that every choice reflects both integrity and responsibility. Balancing the interests of various stakeholders often presents a labyrinth of competing priorities, where the path to fairness is rarely straightforward. In these times, the clarity of one's principles acts as a beacon, guiding decision-makers through the murky waters of potential consequences. By weaving empathy and ethical foresight into their decision-making fabric, leaders can not only inspire trust but also achieve sustainable outcomes that honor the diverse needs of those they impact. It's this ethical consciousness that ultimately empowers individuals to make decisions that stand the test of scrutiny and time, fostering a culture of principled leadership in even the most formidable circumstances.

Navigating Moral Dilemmas

A high-stakes decision-making environment often challenges one's moral compass. When faced with ethical dilemmas, the choices made not only define the immediate outcome but also shape a leader's influence and character. Navigating these complex moral quandaries requires an introspective look at one's core values and a deep understanding of the broader social implications of each decision.

Moral dilemmas often emerge when two or more values come into conflict. For example, a decision that maximizes shareholder profits might contradict the ethical treatment of employees. Such situations demand a nuanced approach where stakeholders must weigh short-term gains against long-term trust and credibility. Leaders can't rely on intuition alone; they need a structured framework to navigate these waters.

The cornerstone of making moral choices starts with clarity. Clarity about personal and organizational values provides a reference point to measure potential decisions. Leaders who consistently align their decisions with clearly defined ethical principles can navigate moral dilemmas more confidently. This alignment not only fosters trust but also serves as a guiding light in turbulent times.

Yet, defining values is only half the battle. Understanding how these values manifest in real-world scenarios requires both reflection and experience. Take, for example, the ethical challenges faced by healthcare professionals during a pandemic. They often have to choose who receives life-saving treatment when resources are limited. Here, values like equity and compassion clash with practical constraints, forcing difficult, sometimes heartbreaking, decisions.

One effective approach to tackling moral dilemmas is scenario-based planning. This involves anticipating potential ethical challenges and envisioning various outcomes before they arise. Role-playing different scenarios, weighing each option's pros and cons, and considering stakeholder perspectives can prepare decision-makers for when real dilemmas strike. In scenarios where no solution seems ethically pure, this preparation can mitigate potential harm and foster transparency.

Leaders should also foster an environment where ethical discourse is encouraged and valued. By nurturing a culture of open dialogue, organizations can ensure that diverse perspectives are considered in decision-making processes. This not only empowers individual team members but also fortifies the organization's ethical standards. Encouraging honest discussions around potential pitfalls and moral gray areas strengthens collective commitment to principled decision-making.

Additionally, leaning on an ethical advisory group can provide valuable insights. These groups, composed of people from varying backgrounds and areas of expertise, can help identify blind spots and offer creative solutions to seemingly intractable problems. By consulting these advisors, leaders can see past their biases and make more informed, equitable decisions.

Laying out a robust ethical framework may seem daunting, but its importance cannot be overstated. A clear set of guiding principles allows leaders to act consistently, even when decisions are fraught with tension and contradictory demands. In practice, this means consistently linking actions to higher goals and justifiable ethical logic, which shines through even under intense scrutiny.

The application of empathy also plays a crucial role in resolving moral dilemmas. Empathy involves understanding and entering into another's feelings, and this can transform decision-making from purely logical to both logical and humane. By stepping into the shoes of those affected, leaders can make decisions that honor the dignity and worth of every individual impacted.

For instance, consider the impact of a decision concerning layoffs during financial hardships. Not only must a leader address the immediate financial needs of the organization but also weigh the personal and societal impacts that such decisions have on individual employees and their families. When empathy guides decisions, they are more likely to resonate positively with all concerned parties, leading to a compassionate and fair approach.

Of course, moral dilemmas don't come with easy solutions. They require striking a balance between conflicting priorities and managing the aftermath of decisions that might not please everyone. Leaders often encounter moral distress—which is the result of knowing the right thing to do but being unable to act owing to various constraints. Recognizing this emotional struggle is an important component of ethical resolution and can lead to richer, more thoughtful decision experiences.

Ultimately, navigating moral dilemmas in high-stakes situations is about more than just making the right call. It's about making decisions that align with one's deepest values and having the courage to stand by them when challenges arise. By cultivating a principled approach, decision-makers can navigate ethical challenges with integrity and inspire others through their example.

As leaders, framing moral dilemmas as opportunities for growth can be transformative. These challenges can teach invaluable lessons about courage, resilience, and the power of ethical leadership. By embracing these difficult choices, we forge a path that leads not only to successful decision-making but also to a legacy of integrity and trust. Moral dilemmas, while daunting, can become pivotal learning moments that shape us into better decision-makers and stronger leaders.

Balancing Stakeholder Interests

In the complex world of high-stakes decisions, balancing stakeholder interests is both an art and a science. Stakeholders can range from employees, customers, and investors to the broader public and regulatory bodies. Each has their own priorities, needs, and sometimes conflicting expectations. When the pressure mounts, and the stakes are high, it's essential to navigate these varying demands with a steady hand and a clear mind.

One of the first steps in balancing these interests is to understand who the stakeholders are and what they value. This requires an empathetic approach—putting oneself in the shoes of others to truly grasp their perspective. A decision that might seem beneficial on the surface may have deep ramifications for a particular group. For instance, cost-cutting measures that enhance short-term profitability might be applauded by investors but can demoralize employees or degrade product quality. It's crucial to engage in active listening and gather input from all affected parties. Doing so not only provides a comprehensive view but also builds trust among stakeholders.

Trust is a crucial currency in decision-making. When stakeholders feel heard and valued, they are more likely to support outcomes, even if they are not entirely in their favor. Hence, open lines of communication are paramount. Regular updates and transparent discussions can help clarify intentions and manage expectations. This can be accomplished through town hall meetings, surveys, or one-on-one discussions, depending on the size and scope of the stakeholder groups.

Another critical aspect is prioritizing stakeholder interests based on the organization's core values and long-term vision. Not all interests will align perfectly with the company's strategic goals. Decision-makers must weigh each interest in terms of its alignment with these goals and its impact on the organization's future. It's helpful to create a stakeholder map categorizing them by their influence and interest levels, which can guide prioritization.

- High-influence, high-interest stakeholders demand immediate attention and careful consideration.

- Low-influence, high-interest groups can be woven into engagement programs, keeping them informed and involved in suitable capacities.

- Conversely, high-influence, low-interest stakeholders might require strategic updates to maintain their potential support when needed.

The ability to navigate ethical dilemmas is a key component of balancing stakeholder interests. These dilemmas often involve situations where two or more ethical principles conflict. For instance, the duty to shareholders might conflict with the environmental stewardship principles that the company stands for. Decisions must be made transparently, acknowledging these conflicts and addressing them openly with stakeholders. Utilizing ethical frameworks or engaging ethics committees can provide guidance and lend credibility to the decision-making process.

Flexibility is equally important. The environment in which decisions are made is often dynamic, with stakeholder expectations and external conditions continuously evolving. This requires an adaptive approach where strategies are revisited and revised as needed. Decision-makers should not fear shifting course if new information or changing circumstances demand it. Demonstrating resilience and a willingness to adapt can transform potential conflicts into opportunities for innovation and growth.

Moreover, genuine empathy and consideration for all stakeholders can inspire loyalty and engagement. Consider a company facing corporate restructuring. By transparently communicating the reasons, objectives, and expected outcomes while actively seeking feedback, leadership can minimize feelings of uncertainty and foster a collective resolve to overcome challenges. This approach can turn adversaries into allies, making stakeholders active participants in the decision-making process rather than passive observers.

The importance of balancing stakeholder interests extends beyond immediate outcomes. Decisions made under high stakes can set precedents and influence the organization's culture. They create ripple effects that affect how society views the organization and its leaders. In this context, decisions become not just about choosing the best course of action in the present, but also about safeguarding the organization's reputation and ensuring its future success.

In conclusion, balancing stakeholder interests is a crucial part of ethical decision-making in high-stakes environments. It requires a keen understanding of stakeholder dynamics, a commitment to core values, transparent communication, and a readiness to embrace ethical complexities. By doing so, decision-makers can ensure that their choices are not only justifiable but also aligned with the broader vision of creating value for all involved. Success in this area demands a level of agility and foresight that drives not only immediate success but also sustainable, long-term growth.

Ultimately, the goal is to create a landscape where stakeholders see themselves as an integral part of the decision-making fabric. When done effectively, balancing stakeholder interests fosters collaboration, engenders trust, and strengthens the moral fiber of the organization, empowering leaders to make decisions that resonate well beyond the boardroom.

Chapter 12: Overcoming Decision Paralysis

Amid the chaos of high-stakes environments, decision paralysis can strike even the most seasoned professionals. It's that unsettling state where options overwhelm, urgency pressures, and the fear of picking the wrong path freezes action. Yet, overcoming this paralysis is not just possible, but essential. Begin by setting aside the myth that decisiveness requires complete certainty. Embrace imperfection and recognize that decisiveness thrives on clarity, not certainty. Prioritize your core objectives and use them as a compass to focus your choices. It's crucial to simplify complex scenarios by breaking them into smaller, more manageable decisions. Engaging in this incremental approach reduces anxiety and builds momentum. Also, impose constraints on decision time to prompt action and prevent over-analysis. Remember, confidence in choices is bolstered by commitment, so trust your judgment, act decisively, and let your learning continue post-decision. Through practice and persistence, you'll find that conquering decision paralysis not only empowers you but also transforms potential pitfalls into platforms for progress.

Techniques to Make Confident Choices

When you're staring down the barrel of a high-pressure decision, it can be paralyzing. The stakes are high, and the weight of making the right choice looms large. But what if making choices, even under intense pressure, could be done with confidence and clarity? Let's explore techniques that can help transform decision paralysis into empowered action.

One powerful way to build confidence in decision-making is to sharpen your focus. By concentrating on what's truly essential and cutting through the noise, you gain clarity. Start by defining your goals in detail. What are you trying to achieve, and why does it matter? This foundational understanding helps to align your decision-making process with your core values, providing a steady compass in turbulent situations.

Once your goals are clear, break down the decision into smaller, more manageable parts. This technique reduces the overwhelming nature of complex situations. Ask yourself: What are the key components of this decision that I need to address? By dissecting the problem, you not only identify critical elements but also make the process of decision-making less daunting.

Visualizing the outcomes of each possible choice can be an effective way to bolster your confidence in decisions. Imagine the different scenarios that could unfold based on your actions. What does success look like? Conversely, what would failure entail? Visualization helps paint a mental picture, making the intangible tangible and allowing you to foresee the consequences of your choices, both good and bad.

Another strategy involves seeking feedback from trusted colleagues or mentors. Discussing your options and the rationale behind them can uncover blind spots and provide new insights. Remember the value of diverse perspectives. They're not just about spotting potential pitfalls—they can inspire innovative solutions you might not have considered.

Asking targeted questions is an invaluable technique. When you frame your decision-making process around a series of clear, direct questions, you can evaluate the problem from various angles. This approach forces you to consider aspects you might otherwise overlook and helps you adjust your decisions based on sound reasoning.

It can be easy to fall into the trap of overthinking. To combat this, set a specific timeframe for your decision-making process. Constraints can enhance creativity and focus. Structure deadlines to foster a sense of urgency that propels you forward, pushing past the inertia of over-analysis.

Practicing mindfulness can strengthen your confidence when making choices. Being mindful helps ground you in the present, reducing the anxiety that stems from dwelling on past failures or future uncertainties. It sharpens your ability to recognize and regulate emotional responses, allowing for clarity and balance in high-pressure moments.

To build a habit of confident decision-making, review past decisions—both good and bad. Analyze the processes and outcomes. What worked, and what didn't? By understanding your patterns, you refine your decision-making capabilities and become more adept at predicting future success.

Embracing intuition as part of your toolkit can also enhance decision-making. While relying solely on gut feelings can be risky, integrating intuition with analytics offers a balanced approach. Your subconscious accumulates knowledge and experience over time, which, when combined with factual data, leads to well-rounded choices.

Visualization, mindfulness, and seeking feedback form a triad that reinforces each other, grounding your process in reality while keeping sight of the larger picture. These techniques foster a deep-seated confidence essential to effective decision-making under pressure.

Lastly, remind yourself that no decision is foolproof. Even with the best techniques, some outcomes are beyond control. Embrace this uncertainty and focus on making the best decision with the information at hand. This mindset reduces fear of failure and empowers you to move forward decisively, equipped with confidence.

In summary, transforming decision paralysis into confident action doesn't happen overnight. It requires intention and practice. These techniques offer a robust framework to navigate high-pressure decisions with clarity, turning what once was a daunting process into an opportunity for growth and success. Confidence isn't just a trait—it's a skill that's honed with every choice made.

Avoiding Over-Analysis

In the relentless pursuit of getting decisions just right, professionals often tumble into the pit of over-analysis. It's a trap that's all too familiar in high-stakes environments where the risk of getting it wrong looms large. Yet, overthinking can be just as hazardous as making a hasty call. The challenge, then, is not merely to gather and scrutinize information but to know when enough is enough—to recognize the tipping point where further analysis serves no constructive purpose and could even hinder effective decision-making.

Over-analysis, or analysis paralysis as it's sometimes known, isn't just about having too much data or too many choices. It's an insidious process where the quest for certainty clashes with the intrinsic uncertainties of life, leading to stagnation. It's tempting to believe that more information will lead to better outcomes, yet there comes a point where collecting more data only adds noise and confusion. Professionals who've mastered decision-making understand that clarity comes not just from thorough analysis but also from setting clear boundaries on how much information is needed to act decisively.

One key strategy to avoid over-analysis is to clearly define the decision criteria up front. By establishing what really matters—whether it's aligning with core values, meeting strategic goals, or balancing risk with opportunity—professionals can anchor their analysis to something concrete. This pre-defined framework acts as a guidepost, preventing them from being swayed by irrelevant details or the endless "what-ifs" that can derail decision processes.

An effective technique borrowed from time management principles is to impose time constraints on decision-making tasks. Setting deadlines forces decisions to be made with the information available at a given moment, rather than waiting for more data. This approach not only curtails over-analysis but also harnesses the positive energy that can come from working under pressure. Interestingly, some of the best decisions arise not from exhaustive deliberation but from a combination of informed intuition and a clear understanding of one's goals and limitations.

Moreover, simplifying complex problems into smaller, manageable parts can be a practical solution. Breaking a daunting decision into smaller components allows for more focused analysis and prevents the mind from feeling overwhelmed. Tackling these less intimidating pieces can give professionals the confidence to progress step-by-step until the larger decision comes into focus, reducing the temptation to over-analyze each component excessively.

Regular reflection is another powerful tool to combat the urge to over-analyze. By periodically stepping back and reviewing the decision-making process, professionals can assess whether they are gathering information with purposeful intent or just endlessly sifting through data in search of elusive certainty. Reflection encourages mindfulness, ensuring that professionals can recalibrate their approach before they veer too far down the rabbit hole of doubt and hesitation.

To foster a mindset that avoids over-analysis, it's crucial to embrace a degree of uncertainty. Recognize that no decision is completely shielded from risk or unforeseen consequences. The ability to accept this while still moving forward is what differentiates effective decision-makers from those held captive by their analysis. Indeed, decision-making is as much an art as it is a science, requiring a balance between meticulous evaluation and decisive action.

Feedback loops are instrumental in refining decision-making processes, minimizing the temptation to over-analyze future decisions. By reviewing outcomes, identifying successes, and understanding missteps, professionals can adjust their strategies. This iterative process cultivates confidence and agility, ensuring decisions are not just well-considered but also contextually aware and adaptable.

Finally, there's an often-overlooked ally in the battle against over-analysis: collaboration. Inviting multiple perspectives not only enriches the decision-making process but also provides natural checks against analysis paralysis. Diverse viewpoints can highlight different priorities and help clarify which aspects of a problem truly merit in-depth consideration and which do not. Collaborative efforts can also reaffirm when a decision path has been sufficiently explored, anchoring teams to move forward with collective confidence.

In essence, avoiding over-analysis requires an intentional balance of rigor and pragmatism. It's about having the courage to act on well-founded conclusions without being paralyzed by the pursuit of perfection. As professionals hone this delicate balance, they equip themselves with a sharper decision-making toolkit, ready to face high-pressure situations with both clarity and resolve.

Ultimately, overcoming the habits of over-analysis is akin to casting off weights that keep decision-makers tethered. With practice and intention, professionals can break free, transforming potentials from mere analysis into decisive actions that drive success. Through defining criteria, setting boundaries, embracing uncertainty, and leveraging collaboration, the journey to effective and empowering decision-making becomes not just possible, but a reality.

Chapter 13: Mastering Crisis Management

In the heart of chaos, the ability to master crisis management becomes the pivotal point for making decisions that can turn a potential disaster into a triumph. To navigate the storm of a crisis, one must not only develop strategic response plans but also foster an adaptable mindset for real-time problem-solving. This requires a balance of foresight and flexibility, marrying preemptive planning with the agility to pivot when the unexpected strikes. By cultivating a culture of preparedness and resilience, leaders can transform high-pressure environments into arenas of opportunity. Crisis management isn't just about survival; it's about emerging on the other side stronger and wiser. In these moments, the convergence of clear communication, decisive action, and a calm demeanor sets the path toward successful outcomes, creating a legacy of reliability and confidence in decision-making.

Developing Crisis Response Plans

Crisis response plans are the anchor that holds steady in the turbulent waters of high-stakes decision-making. Developing an effective plan requires clear foresight, strategic thinking, and an acute awareness of potential risks. When facing a crisis, the power of preparation is immeasurable; it's the critical difference between being reactive and proactive. The formulation of such plans isn't merely about ironing out logistics or forming a checklist of tasks. It's about crafting a framework designed to guide you through chaos with clarity and confidence.

At the heart of any successful crisis response plan is a deep understanding of the specific context within which decisions are being made. Not all crises are created equal, and understanding the unique pressures of each situation can help tailor an appropriate response. This process involves identifying the key pressure points and potential trigger events that could escalate a situation. By dissecting these elements, you'll be better equipped to anticipate the various paths a crisis could take and prepare accordingly. This requires thinking several moves ahead and visualizing possible outcomes, both positive and negative.

Effective crisis response plans integrate a robust communication strategy. Clear communication serves as the lifeline during critical moments, ensuring that vital information flows seamlessly across all levels of an organization or team. It's not just about what is communicated but how it's conveyed. The tone, medium, and timing of communication can significantly affect the outcomes of a crisis management effort. Therefore, defining channels and establishing protocols for consistent messaging become key components of the response plan. This extends to both internal stakeholders and external audiences, ensuring transparency and maintaining trust when it matters most.

Another cornerstone of resilient crisis management is adaptability. While having a detailed plan is essential, flexibility should be built into its core. The capacity to pivot and recalibrate as situations evolve can mean the difference between seizing an opportunity or suffering a setback. Crafting scenarios and running simulations can prepare decision-makers for a range of possible realities, encouraging agile thinking and rapid adjustment under pressure. This is where the blend of data-driven insights and intuitive judgment becomes invaluable, as new information can radically alter perceptions and subsequent decisions.

Once a crisis response plan is drafted, it's crucial to ensure that all key stakeholders are not just aware of it but actively familiar. Regular training sessions and drills are not optional; they're necessary exercises that turn theoretical plans into muscle memory. These practices instill confidence and facilitate swift, assured actions when time is of the essence. Creating a culture where team members feel empowered to voice their insights and concerns also leads to stronger, more comprehensive plans. Decision-making shouldn't occur in a vacuum; rather, it should be the result of collaborative and inclusive processes.

Furthermore, crisis response isn't a one-time effort. Plans must be living documents, continually reviewed and updated to reflect changing conditions and new learnings. After a crisis has passed, the debrief is just as critical as the preparation. Analyzing what went right and identifying areas for improvement can strengthen future responses. By fostering a mindset that embraces learning and adaptability, you'll not only build a more resilient crisis management framework but also enhance overall decision-making capabilities.

Empathy, too, plays a vital role within crisis management. A human-centered approach can create more meaningful connections and deliver more effective responses. Understanding and responding to the emotional landscape of all involved—whether it's team members, customers, or other stakeholders—can promote trust and foster collaboration. In high-pressure environments, it's essential to balance operational imperatives with personal sensitivities.

Ultimately, the goal of developing crisis response plans is to empower decision-makers to thrive under pressure. By formulating strong foundations, leveraging robust communication, promoting adaptability, engaging stakeholders, and embracing continuous improvement, you're not just preparing for potential crises—you're cultivating a proactive, decisive mindset capable of overcoming challenges and seizing opportunities in equal measure.

Real-Time Problem Solving

In the heart of a crisis, decision-making becomes an art of instant judgments, where speed and agility are as critical as accuracy. Professionals face an array of challenges that demand more than mere strategy; they call for intuition, adaptability, and resilience. Real-time problem solving is about the ability not only to make decisions amid chaos but also to pivot when the unexpected occurs.

Crisis scenarios are often fluid, evolving in ways that require a dynamic approach. The capacity to read the room and anticipate what's coming next can distinguish successful crisis managers from those who falter. It's about staying one step ahead, understanding that real-time doesn't just mean rapid—it also means appropriate. Having a framework to rely on is essential, yet maintaining flexibility allows you to deviate and innovate when necessary.

To manage crises effectively, you need to prioritize the immediacy of decisions while considering long-term impacts. This starts with rapid data assessment—identifying what information is critical and what's extraneous. Access to data is abundant, but in the heat of the moment, discernment is key. The ability to quickly filter noise from significance enables leaders to focus on actionable insights.

Consider the role of a calm mind in the storm of crisis. Stress and anxiety can cloud judgment, leading to hasty decisions. Therefore, ensuring clarity of thought becomes paramount. Techniques such as deep breathing or brief mental pauses can stabilize the mind, allowing more grounded decision-making processes. Real-time problem solving isn't about emotions taking over, but rather harnessing them as tools for better judgment.

In situations where time is a luxury, decision-makers must leverage their team's collective knowledge. Engaging the right people at the right moments brings diverse perspectives into play. This collaboration can present new angles and innovative solutions that might not have been visible from an individual standpoint. Effective leaders encourage input and feedback, creating an environment where team members feel valued and empowered to contribute.

Collaboration extends beyond the internal team and into external resources and networks. Relationships established before a crisis can provide pivotal insights during critical moments. Whether it's industry peers or subject-matter experts, others can offer perspectives that help shape more effective decisions. Developing and maintaining these connections before a crisis arises is crucial, so they can be mobilized swiftly when required.

Of course, even the best-laid plans encounter unforeseen hurdles. Here, a solution-focused mindset becomes vital. Instead of fixating on what's not working, efficient problem solvers reframe challenges as opportunities for innovation. Thought leaders in crisis management often focus on 'what can be done' rather than 'what went wrong,' redirecting the conversation towards actionable pathways forward.

Flexibility is another essential component of real-time problem solving. When initial strategies falter, agile leaders pivot rather than persistently sticking to a failing course. For example, if a planned communication strategy isn't resonating with its audience, adjusting the approach rapidly can prevent the situation from escalating further. Adapting on the fly ensures that momentum is maintained, and efforts remain effective.

This section wouldn't be complete without underlining the importance of post-crisis analysis. Once the immediate situation is under control, it's critical to review and learn from the decisions made. Reflecting on what worked allows you to solidify successful strategies, whereas understanding missteps provides valuable lessons for the future. Such reflective practices contribute to an evolving skill set that enhances future real-time problem solving.

Technology, while not the panacea, plays a supporting role in this fast-paced environment. Digital tools and platforms can accelerate data gathering and processing, offering decision-makers real-time analytics that ground their judgment in tangible evidence. However, technology should augment rather than replace innate human judgment. The human element, with its empathy and emotional intelligence, remains irreplaceable in navigating crises.

In conclusion, real-time problem solving in crisis management is not purely about making fast decisions. It involves setting up systems for efficient information processing, maintaining flexibility, fostering collaboration, and applying a cool-headed approach that integrates both intuition and analysis. As you master these skills, you'll find yourself not just weathering the storm but steering your ship confidently through it.

Chapter 14: Learning from Mistakes and Failures

In the high-pressure arena, where choices can make or break outcomes, learning from mistakes and failures becomes a critical skill. Embracing setbacks as learning opportunities fuels growth and transformation, rather than halting progress. It's about examining past decisions with a keen eye, distinguishing between calculated risks and missteps. This reflection isn't an exercise in self-reproach but an essential analysis that constructs a bridge to better judgment. With each failure dissected, professionals gain insight into what worked, what didn't, and, most importantly, why. The process nurtures resilience and innovation, ensuring that failure is not a terminal event but a catalyst for rejuvenating strategies. By adopting this mindset, high-stakes decision-makers can pivot swiftly, turning potential derailments into stepping stones. Building a resilient psyche doesn't just happen; it's crafted through the iterative dance of risk, failure, analysis, and adaptation, fortifying a decision-maker's ability to thrive under stress.

Analyzing Past Decisions

Reflecting upon past decisions is not an exercise in self-flagellation but rather a critical component of personal and professional growth. This process, albeit sometimes uncomfortable, offers invaluable insights into our cognitive processes and emotional reactions. By analyzing past decisions, especially those made under pressure, professionals can refine their decision-making skills, fortify their resilience, and gain a clearer understanding of what strategies work best in high-stakes situations.

When delving into past decisions, it's important to approach the exercise with both objectivity and empathy. Objectivity allows you to assess the decision without the burden of emotional bias, considering the facts as they were at the time. Empathy, on the other hand, permits you to appreciate the emotional state you were in, as well as any external pressures that might have influenced the outcome. Together, these perspectives provide a balanced view, facilitating constructive learning rather than unnecessary regret.

Consider starting with a decision journal. Document each significant decision, noting the context, the options considered, the decision made, and the outcome. Over time, patterns will emerge, revealing tendencies and areas for improvement. Are you overly cautious? Do you give too much weight to gut feelings at the expense of data? Identifying these patterns is the first step in understanding your decision-making process, helping you to recalibrate and fine-tune your approach for future scenarios.

Ask yourself comprehensive questions when reviewing past decisions. What were the key factors that influenced your choice? Were there alternative options that you overlooked? Would the outcome have been different if another path was chosen? These questions serve to deepen your understanding, moving beyond surface-level analysis to uncover the underlying drivers of your decisions. This approach mirrors the scientific method, where you form hypotheses, test them and analyze the results to gain insights.

Another powerful tool is retrospection in a team setting. It allows for obtaining diverse perspectives, which enriches the analysis. When team members share their views on a collective decision, it unveils biases and dynamics that might have gone unnoticed. Assembling a group to dissect a past project is not about shouldering blame. It's about elucidating lessons in a collaborative way, fostering a shared narrative of growth.

While analyzing, remember that time itself is a valuable teacher. Some lessons only become clear with the passage of time, as hindsight offers a clarity that was not possible in the moment. The outcome of a decision may initially seem negative, but with time, it might reveal itself as a blessing in disguise. Being open to this unfolding perspective can transform how you view failure and success, encouraging you to remain patient and receptive to long-term insights.

Moreover, balance humility with confidence. It's easy to dwell on poor decisions, chastising yourself for perceived failures. Instead, view them as an opportunity to cultivate humility and reinforce your resolve. Recognize that mistakes are an inevitable aspect of risk-taking and innovation. Confidence stems from knowing that each decision, right or wrong, edges you closer to becoming a more proficient decision-maker who is not paralyzed by past errors, but rather emboldened by them.

Expanding your knowledge base through literature, expert advice, or workshops can provide fresh perspectives and techniques. Learn from the narratives of leaders who've faced similar dilemmas. Their experiences can offer strategic methodologies and highlight the universality of certain challenges, reducing the isolation often felt in high-pressure decision environments.

Sometimes, despite the best analysis, past decisions will remain shrouded in ambiguity. Accepting this ambiguity is key; being comfortable with not knowing everything fosters an adaptive mindset. It stimulates creativity and innovation, as you learn to pivot and adjust, crafting new paths with the wisdom gained from previous endeavors.

Ultimately, the art of analyzing past decisions lies in the balance of introspection and action. It's an ongoing, dynamic process that shapes your future strategies while respecting past experiences. As you internalize these lessons, your repertoire of skills expands, equipping you with the knowledge and resilience to navigate the complexities of future high-stakes decision-making with increased assurance and efficacy.

Transforming Setbacks into Opportunities

In the high-stakes realm of professional decision-making, setbacks are inevitable. However, they're not the end of the road. Instead, they can be invaluable catalysts for personal and professional growth. The ability to transform these setbacks into opportunities can set the truly successful apart from the rest. It's a skill that requires both perspective and perseverance, starting with the understanding that setbacks are a natural part of the decision-making landscape.

Let's consider the foundational concept that each mistake contains a seed of learning. When faced with a failure, it's essential to engage with it constructively. This requires moving beyond the initial sting of disappointment or embarrassment and instead focusing on what the experience can teach. Essentially, it's about reframing failure from a negative endpoint to a step in a continuous journey of improvement. By doing so, we cultivate resilience and prepare ourselves to tackle future challenges with enhanced strategies.

Resilience isn't just bouncing back—it's bouncing forward, carrying the hard-earned lessons gleaned from adversity. Professionals who thrive under pressure often view setbacks as training opportunities for future situations. They foster a growth mindset, understanding that the road to success is paved with trials that offer insights into personal and organizational weaknesses. With this mindset, setbacks become opportunities to refine skills, adjust strategies, and strengthen decision-making processes.

Analyzing the root causes of a setback is crucial. Often, failures stem from misjudged risks or overlooked details. By systematically dissecting past decisions without assigning blame, professionals can uncover the underlying issues that need addressing. Was it a miscalculation in risk assessment? Did cognitive biases cloud judgment? Was the communication in the decision-making process unclear? Each question answered is an opportunity for strengthening future decisions.

Once the causes are understood, it's time to innovate. Setbacks can spark creativity by forcing us to think outside the box and explore unconventional methods for solving issues. This is where the transformative power of failure lies: it unlocks doors to new pathways and solutions that might not have been considered in the comfort of success. Encouraging a culture of experimentation and innovation—nurtured by the lessons of failure—empowers teams and individuals to push boundaries and venture into uncharted territories with confidence.

Let's not overlook the invaluable role of feedback during these moments. Constructive feedback from peers, mentors, and even internal reflection plays a pivotal role in learning from setbacks. They provide external perspectives that can reveal blind spots, offering insights that are sometimes difficult to uncover in isolation. Encouragement to seek out and actively engage in feedback loops ensures that lessons from failures are well-absorbed and adequately applied in future scenarios.

It's also vital to align learning from setbacks with core values and long-term objectives. This alignment acts as a compass that guides decision-makers in using failures to reinforce their commitment to sustainable success. When failures are interpreted in the context of overarching goals, they become stepping stones rather than stumbling blocks. This process strengthens the resolve to pursue objectives with clarity and purpose.

While failure can often feel like an isolated event, sharing experiences within a team can be particularly powerful. It reinforces that making mistakes is a shared human experience and fosters a supportive environment where individuals feel safe to learn openly. This culture of transparency does more than transform setbacks—it equips teams to anticipate potential pitfalls and preemptively strategize for future challenges.

Emotional intelligence plays a crucial role in leveraging setbacks into opportunities. Recognizing and managing emotions during times of failure are critical in maintaining focus on learning outcomes. It allows professionals to detach from the personal affront of failure and zero in on the practical steps needed to convert current challenges into future successes.

The most profound successes often come from those who have weathered significant failures. Each setback is not just an opportunity to learn but a chance to innovate, rejuvenate, and reimagine the path ahead. As we move forward, integrating these experiences continues to build the toolkit of an effective decision-maker, enhancing their ability to think critically, act decisively, and thrive in high-stakes environments.

In essence, setbacks should never be seen as barriers but as bridges to greater achievements. By nurturing a mindset that embraces failure as a vital component of the decision-making process, professionals can position themselves not just to survive but to thrive in the face of adversity. This is how we transform setbacks into opportunities—not merely by enduring them but by extracting their full potential to elevate our paths to success.

Chapter 15: The Role of Creativity in Decision-Making

In the realm of high-stakes decisions, where pressure can mount quickly, creativity often acts as a crucial ally. It's not just about thinking outside the box; it's about expanding the box, reshaping how we perceive problems and solutions. Creative thinking underpins innovative breakthroughs, not by following a linear path, but by encouraging unexpected connections and radical ideas. When facing complex challenges, professionals can benefit from harnessing creativity to explore possibilities that aren't immediately obvious, creating opportunities for transformative decisions. Instead of relying solely on conventional wisdom, the infusion of creative processes allows decision-makers to navigate uncertainties and pressures with newfound clarity and adaptability. This dynamic mindset turns pressure into a catalyst for innovation, invigorating decision-making with fresh perspectives and the courage to embrace original solutions. By actively integrating creativity into decision-making processes, individuals not only enhance their ability to solve problems but also cultivate a resourceful approach that leads to superior outcomes even when the stakes are high.

Innovative Thinking During Pressure

In the labyrinth of high-pressure scenarios, our ability to think innovatively can be the compass that guides us to effective decision-making. It's often in moments of crisis that creative solutions emerge, where conventional paths fall short.

Consider a team facing a critical deadline, with their project hanging by a thread due to unforeseen circumstances. While stress levels surge, innovative thinking can transform obstacles into stepping stones. It's about diving deep into the recesses of one's mind and drawing upon a mix of experience, intuition, and inspiration. When time constraints tighten, creative thinking allows leaders to adapt and pivot, turning potential failures into breakthroughs.

Historical examples illustrate that many groundbreaking ideas were born under immense pressure. For instance, during the Apollo 13 mission, NASA engineers had to come up with a rapid solution to bring the astronauts back to Earth safely after a disastrous oxygen tank explosion. Under such extreme circumstances, the team had no other choice but to think outside the box, leading to one of the most innovative problem-solving efforts in history.

Pressure can trigger a response in our brain rendering us either focused or frantic. It's a fine line, and walking it requires an understanding of both our psychological and emotional landscapes. Creative thinking under duress is more than just a skill; it's an art form that combines knowledge, experience, and imagination.

The key is to find that perfect balance where stress becomes a motivational tool rather than a hindrance. A stressful situation can ignite a sense of urgency that stimulates the brain, pushing it to be more alert, attentive, and ready to devise novel solutions. However, letting stress take control can equally lead to a mental block, clouding judgment and suppressing creative thought.

One strategy to foster innovative thinking under pressure is to create mental space. Psychological research suggests that simple techniques such as deep breathing, temporarily removing oneself from the environment, even if just mentally, or engaging in brief meditative practices can help clear the mind.

Another approach is using *lateral thinking*, a term popularized by Edward de Bono. Lateral thinking involves seeking solutions through an indirect and creative approach, often through viewing the problem from a number of angles. It encourages looking beyond the obvious and challenges assumptions, which can lead to unexpected and effective solutions.

Picture a basketball coach in the final seconds of a tied championship game. Under immense pressure, the coach draws upon years of experience and creative strategies, but instead of sticking solely to the game plan, he improvises a play that may just catch the opposing team off-guard. This ability to improvise, to think on their feet, often originates from a space of calm in the chaos.

To cultivate innovative thinking during pressure, leaders can also embrace constraints to fuel creativity. Paradoxically, working within limitations can inspire teams to stretch their imaginations, to find new avenues and methods, which they wouldn't have explored within a 'business-as-usual' scenario.

Moreover, encouraging a culture that values creativity and acceptance of failure can liberate team members to take risks. In a company where unconventional ideas are welcomed and examined rather than dismissed outright, employees feel more empowered to brainstorm freely, even when the stakes are high.

The crucial aspect of these brainstorming sessions is to keep the energy positive and the environment judgment-free. Doing so ensures that everyone feels comfortable sharing their thoughts, no matter how wild they may seem initially. The best ideas often sprout from the seeds of the most daring and seemingly outlandish suggestions.

Collaboration also plays a pivotal role in fostering innovative thinking under pressure. Tapping into the diverse perspectives of a team can produce a wealth of ideas, from which the most viable solutions can be selected. As seen in many corporate and business settings, when team members with varied experiences and expertise come together, the sum of their parts often exceeds their individual contributions.

Take the example of cross-disciplinary teams in institutions like Google or IDEO, where employees from different backgrounds are encouraged to collaborate on projects. The resulting fusion of disciplines frequently leads to unique solutions that one field alone might not achieve.

In the end, innovative thinking during pressure is about daring to be different. It's not just about what you know, but how you think—how you connect the dots differently, how you question the status quo, and how you envision possibilities others overlook. With practice, this way of thinking becomes not just second nature but an invaluable asset as one navigates the choppy waters of critical decision-making.

Remember that innovation is a skill that can be honed. As high-pressure decisions become routine, the flair for creativity becomes more than just a reaction; it becomes a proactive strategy. It sets apart those who merely endure pressure from those who thrive in it, crafting solutions that lead to success.

Brainstorming Techniques

Creativity thrives in an environment that encourages exploration and open-mindedness. Brainstorming, as a tool, acts as a bridge between chaos and order, a conduit for thoughts to transform into actionable ideas. Cultivating effective brainstorming techniques is essential not just for generating creative solutions, but for honing decision-making skills under pressure. Variability in brainstorming sessions—their structure, participants, and methods—invites diverse perspectives, which are critical in high-stakes situations.

One of the most effective techniques for brainstorming is the classic "no judgment" rule. By separating the generation of ideas from the evaluation phase, the creative process can unfold unencumbered. This approach encourages wild and unconventional ideas to emerge, unrestrained by immediate criticism or feasibility concerns. In the context of decision-making, this freedom often uncovers innovative solutions that wouldn't surface in a more constrained setting.

However, it's not enough just to let ideas flow freely. Structure within brainstorming is pivotal. Techniques like the "Six Thinking Hats" by Edward de Bono encourage looking at a problem from multiple angles. Each "hat" represents a different perspective—fact-based, emotional, creative, and so on—helping decision-makers to thoroughly evaluate a scenario. By systematically exploring a decision's facets, individuals not only develop a rounded view of the problem but also enrich their capacity for creativity.

In addition to structured methods, tools like mind mapping use visual connections to unlock creative potential. By diagramming thoughts and ideas, participants can see connections that are less apparent through linear methods. This technique is particularly useful for those who think visually, allowing them to organize and relate ideas in a non-linear fashion. Mind mapping fosters a more holistic approach that can lead to revelations about unexpected correlations.

Engaging in brainstorming sessions with diverse groups can exponentially enhance the richness of ideas generated. A mix of varying expertise, backgrounds, and cultural perspectives can break down homogenous thought patterns that often stifle creativity. The diversity of input inherently broadens the pool of strategies and solutions, preparing decision-makers to tackle challenges with a more eclectic toolkit.

While diversity is key, it's equally crucial to cultivate an environment where participants feel safe to share freely. Psychological safety in teams encourages vulnerability and authenticity, which are vital for bold creativity. Leaders must ensure that every voice is heard and valued, regardless of rank or experience. This inclusivity can serve as a catalyst, promoting an atmosphere where groundbreaking ideas can thrive unchallenged by fear of ridicule or dismissal.

Asynchronous brainstorming is another strategy worth exploring, particularly in a world where virtual collaboration is common. Tools like shared documents or virtual whiteboards allow participants to contribute ideas on their own schedules, reducing the pressure that can come with real-time sessions. This method also gives introverts, who might be less forthcoming in live settings, the opportunity to share ideas without the immediacy of group settings.

Over time, incorporating feedback loops into brainstorming sessions can refine and enhance the creativity process. By analyzing past sessions—what worked, what didn't, and which techniques yielded the best results—teams can continuously tune their approach. This analytical process not only improves future sessions but empowers participants to build on past experiences, leading to more efficient and effective decision-making under pressure.

Another innovative technique is reverse brainstorming, where participants start by focusing on how to achieve the opposite of what is desired. This strategy can reveal obstacles and risk areas, serving as a formidable tool for identifying underlying issues that might otherwise go unnoticed. Recognizing barriers can illuminate new paths, offering fresh angles from which to approach problem-solving and decision-making.

Furthermore, blending techniques such as SCAMPER (Substitute, Combine, Adapt, Modify, Put to another use, Eliminate, and Reverse) transforms existing ideas into something novel. This process encourages creative expansion and reassessment of problems, fostering an environment ripe for ingenuity. By applying this technique, decision-makers can unlock potential solutions and generate ideas that might have initially seemed improbable.

As brainstorming becomes more refined, the capacity to innovate under pressure increases. It is this transformation that turns creativity into a potent ally for decision-makers. Equipped with a suite of techniques—from standard to unconventional—individuals and teams are better positioned to harness creativity when it matters most. In high-stakes environments, where time is often limited and pressure is high, these refined techniques ensure that decision-makers remain adaptable, inventive, and, above all, effective.

While structured brainstorming is invaluable, spontaneous, unstructured brainstorming sessions can also be beneficial. These sessions foster spontaneity, allowing ideas to bubble up organically. Without predefined constraints, participants may discover raw, initial ideas that spur further innovative thinking. It's like planting seeds that might eventually grow into strong and viable decisions.

Ultimately, the goal of brainstorming in decision-making is to cultivate a space where creativity is not just welcomed but harnessed strategically to produce effective solutions. By valuing and employing diverse brainstorming techniques, we transform potential into reality, courageously facing the ambiguities high-stakes decisions bring. We become not just decision-makers but architects of solutions, shaping the outcomes that decide the future.

Chapter 16: Building a Supportive Decision-Making Environment

In high-pressure scenarios, the environment in which decisions are made can be just as critical as the decision itself. Creating a supportive decision-making environment is about fostering a landscape where collaboration thrives and trust acts as a cornerstone. It's about designing a space where team members feel empowered to voice diverse perspectives, knowing their insights are valued and respected. When people trust each other, they're more inclined to take necessary risks, leading to innovative solutions that might not emerge in a more rigid setting. By nurturing a culture of openness and encouraging mutual respect, leaders can ensure that their teams work cohesively, making calculated decisions with confidence and clarity even under the most intense pressure. Ultimately, when collaboration and trust coalesce, the outcome is a robust framework that not only bolsters individual decision-making but also enhances the collective wisdom of the team.

Fostering Collaboration

In the dynamic world of high-stakes decision-making, fostering collaboration is not just beneficial—it's essential. A supportive decision-making environment thrives on the collective intelligence of its members, providing a rich tapestry of perspectives and insights. Collaboration can be the difference between a decision viewed from a single angle and one that is multi-dimensional, taking into account the diverse skills and experiences available in a team.

At the heart of successful collaboration lies communication. Clear and open lines of communication foster trust and transparency, allowing team members to feel valued and heard. When individuals are encouraged to share their thoughts and ideas freely, it often leads to more robust and well-considered decisions. In high-pressure situations, fostering an atmosphere where everyone feels comfortable expressing dissenting opinions can unveil risks and possibilities that might otherwise remain hidden.

To build this environment of collaboration, leaders must be intentional about creating spaces where dialogue is encouraged. Regular meetings shouldn't just focus on checking off a list but should be arenas where brainstorming is welcome. This entails not only listening to the voices that usually dominate discussions but actively seeking the input of quieter team members whose insights might be crucial yet overlooked. A collaborative decision-making process recognizes that every voice adds value.

Moreover, fostering collaboration requires acknowledging the cognitive biases that can impede effective teamwork. It's not uncommon for individuals to gravitate towards those they agree with or to be distracted by confirmation bias. As a leader, cultivating awareness around these biases can help teams remain open-minded. Encouraging diversity in thought and approach can be pivotal in challenging these biases and ensuring that decision-making processes aren't skewed by unexamined presumptions.

Consider the role of emotional intelligence in fostering collaboration. High emotional intelligence allows team members to manage their emotions, alleviate tensions, and build stronger interpersonal relationships. This can lead to more cohesive teams that can navigate the intricacies of decision-making under duress. Leaders who model empathy, remain calm and collected in challenging times, and who celebrate the team's collective achievements can foster a more connected and committed group.

Collaboration also relies heavily on the collective understanding of common goals. It's important that all team members are aware of and aligned with the strategic objectives guiding their decisions. When each individual sees how their contributions tie into the larger organizational vision, it provides a sense of purpose and shared effort, crucial for seamless collaboration.

However, challenges to collaboration are inevitable. Conflicts may arise, and differing priorities can cause friction. To mitigate these, it's beneficial to establish clear roles and responsibilities. When individuals know what's expected of them and how their tasks integrate with others' work, it minimizes ambiguity and enhances mutual respect. Establishing a framework for decision-making that outlines how input is valued, how decisions are finalized, and how disagreements are resolved can streamline the process.

We can't overlook the role of technology in fostering collaboration. In today's world, teams often span continents and time zones. Utilizing collaborative tools and platforms can help maintain fluid communication and ensure everyone stays informed and engaged. Whether it's shared digital workspaces or instant messaging apps, technology enables us to bridge geographical divides and synchronize efforts despite physical distances.

Ultimately, fostering collaboration is a continuous process of learning and adaptation. It requires a mindset that sees every interaction as an opportunity to strengthen team cohesion and collective intelligence. Encourage feedback, reflect on processes, and be willing to make necessary adjustments. By nurturing a culture of collaboration, organizations not only enhance their decision-making capabilities but also set the stage for innovation and sustained success in high-pressure environments.

In summation, fostering collaboration is about more than just teamwork; it's about creating an inclusive atmosphere where each member feels empowered to contribute meaningfully. This approach not only expands the decision-making possibilities but cultivates a culture where insights are shared freely, strategies are developed collectively, and outcomes are enriched by the diverse tapestry of perspectives. As collaboration becomes the backbone of supportive decision-making environments, organizations are better equipped to navigate the complexities of high-stakes landscapes with confidence and agility.

Cultivating Trust Within Teams

Building a supportive decision-making environment isn't just about the mechanics of decision-making—it's equally about the relationships that bind a team together. Trust is the bedrock upon which collaborative success stands. Without it, communication falters, ideas stagnate, and the risk of failure looms larger. Cultivating trust within teams involves a deliberate set of strategies designed to empower individuals and unify efforts toward common goals.

Trust begins with openness. When team leaders and members alike share their thoughts, motives, and concerns transparently, it sets a tone of honesty and integrity. This transparency doesn't just enhance understanding; it encourages everyone to bring their authentic selves to the table. In high-stakes scenarios, knowing that your teammates are genuine in their intentions can provide the assurance needed to be bold in decision-making. It all starts with creating a space where people feel safe to express themselves without fear of judgment.

Listening is another critical component. It's not enough to simply hear words; one must actively engage with what is being communicated. In doing so, team members demonstrate that they value each other's contributions, fostering a sense of mutual respect. Effective listening involves patience and empathy. It's about asking clarifying questions and ensuring you truly grasp the essence of what's being shared. When individuals feel understood, they're more likely to trust their teammates in the decision-making process.

Additionally, trust is fortified through accountability. Holding oneself and others responsible for their roles in the team not only reinforces personal integrity but also ensures that everyone is pulling in the same direction. When accountability is aligned with compassion, mistakes become learning opportunities rather than sources of blame. This shift in perspective can transform setbacks into stepping stones, driving teams forward with resilience and adaptability.

The role of feedback in cultivating trust cannot be understated. Constructive feedback should be integral to team culture. It's about providing insights that help elevate performance while also being open to receiving criticism. Trust deepens when team members know they can rely on each other for honest feedback that's aimed at improvement, not punishment. The key lies in delivering this feedback in a way that is respectful and supportive.

Diversifying team efforts is another effective trust-building strategy. When team members collaborate on various projects or rotate roles, they gain a more comprehensive understanding of their peers' skills and challenges. This exposure helps in recognizing the innate value each member brings, further solidifying trust as team dynamics are better appreciated and respected.

A supportive decision-making environment is greatly bolstered by clear and honest communication. This doesn't only mean effectively conveying decisions but also ensuring that there is a shared understanding of team objectives, strategies, and values. Establishing a common language and set of principles guides decision-making consistency, minimizing misunderstandings and the potential for conflict.

Mutual support and collaboration are at the heart of enhancing trust. By encouraging team members to rely on one another's strengths, innovation and creative problem-solving can flourish. It's about creating an environment where collaboration is not only encouraged but rewarded, recognizing that the sum of a team's capabilities far surpasses its individual parts.

Trust is also about creating a space for vulnerability. Teams must be seen as safe zones where members can express doubts, ask questions, and admit mistakes without fear of negative repercussions. By allowing room for vulnerability, teams can foster a deeper connection among members, leading to increased confidence in their collaborative endeavors.

Finally, celebrating successes collectively strengthens team bonds. Acknowledging both individual and team achievements fosters a culture of recognition and appreciation. This kind of affirmation bolsters morale, driving teams to strive for excellence and enhancing trust in future decision-making processes.

To cultivate trust within teams, it's essential to foster an environment where shared goals are prioritized over individual gain. When team members see themselves as parts of a cohesive whole, driven by a unified vision, trust naturally follows. With trust as the cornerstone, teams are better equipped to navigate the complexities of high-pressure decision-making, leading to outcomes that are both successful and sustainable.

The process of building trust is continuous, requiring commitment from every team member. It's a living construct that evolves with every decision made and every challenge faced. When trust is cultivated effectively within a team, it becomes a powerful driver of success, ensuring that even in the most high-pressure scenarios, decisions are made with confidence and clarity.

Chapter 17: Decision-Making Tools and Technologies

In this age of rapid technological advancement, the tools at our disposal for decision-making are not just abundant but transformative. The advent of sophisticated software and apps designed for strategic decisions offers professionals the ability to analyze complex data sets, forecast outcomes, and visualize the impact of potential choices with unprecedented clarity. Yet, technology's role isn't merely to automate or simplify; it's to augment our intuition and expertise, allowing us to harness data-driven insights while navigating the intricate web of human judgment under pressure. It's crucial to evaluate technology's impact not only on accuracy and efficiency but also on our capacity to remain agile and empathetic in the face of high-stakes decisions. By judiciously integrating these tools, decision-makers can transform challenges into opportunities, paving their way to informed, confident, and impactful outcomes. Embracing these innovations, while staying grounded in our experiences and instincts, is the balanced approach to thriving in an ever-evolving landscape.

Software and Apps for Strategic Decisions

In today's fast-paced business environment, the pressure to make informed and strategic decisions is unrelenting. Decisions must be swift, yet they can't be reckless—that's where software and apps come into play. These technological tools aren't just conveniences; they're essential instruments that augment our decision-making capabilities, providing clarity amidst complexity and a pathway through pressure.

The right software can transform how a professional approaches a decision. At the foundational level, decision-support systems (DSS) offer structured solutions designed to streamline the decision-making process. By gathering, processing, and analyzing vast amounts of data, these systems can highlight trends, forecast outcomes, and deliver insights that might otherwise be obscured by information overload. They're like having a silent partner requiring neither rest nor respite, ever ready to crunch numbers and project scenarios.

Take, for instance, business intelligence (BI) platforms. These applications pull data from various sources, synthesizing it into dashboards and visualizations that are easy to interpret. A top executive can glance at a BI dashboard and, within moments, have a real-time snapshot of their company's performance metrics, customer behavior, or market trends. It's like having a crystal ball—but one rooted in data rather than divination.

Then there are more specialized tools like project management applications, which are indispensable when decisions involve coordinating team efforts, resources, and timelines. With software like Monday.com, Trello, or Asana, projects can be meticulously planned, tasks assigned, and progress tracked all in one place. This kind of visibility ensures that decisions regarding deadlines, resource allocation, and prioritization are informed by real-time insights, not assumptions.

Data analytics often takes center stage in decision-making, and rightly so. However, not all decisions can rely solely on quantitative data. Sometimes, qualitative insights are equally crucial, especially regarding customer feedback and market sentiment. That's where tools like Qualtrics or SurveyMonkey come into play. These platforms help gather and analyze human feedback, ensuring that decisions consider both the numbers and the nuanced emotions and opinions that numbers can't always capture.

The increasing reliance on software extends into simulation tools, which are invaluable in high-pressure scenarios. These applications allow decision-makers to model different scenarios and test the outcomes of various choices without real-world risks. It's akin to conducting dress rehearsals for a high-stakes performance, ensuring every potential outcome is understood before the curtain rises.

Moreover, predictive analytics tools are revolutionizing decision-making by offering foresight based on patterns and statistical probabilities. They provide a glimpse into future trends and behaviors, allowing leaders to anticipate changes and adapt strategies proactively. With platforms like SAP Analytics Cloud or IBM Watson Analytics, businesses are not just reacting to what has happened but preparing for what might happen—a crucial capability in dynamic environments.

It's important, though, to maintain a balance between reliance on technology and human intuition. Software can process information and suggest pathways, but the final decision often requires the human touch—the ability to weigh nuances, consider ethical implications, and integrate overarching goals and core values. An over-reliance on technology without considering human judgment can lead to decisions that may be efficient but lack empathy or long-term vision.

In industries where time is of the essence, apps are bridging the gap between speed and accuracy in decision-making. Mobile applications enable executives to access critical data and analytics while on the move, ensuring decision-making continuity no matter where they are. This agility in information accessibility cannot be overstated, especially in sectors like logistics, finance, or even healthcare, where decisions can be a matter of profits or losses—or life and death.

Yet, as we integrate more technology into our decision-making processes, the importance of cybersecurity and data protection grows. Decision-makers must be vigilant about securing sensitive data to maintain trust and assure stakeholders of the integrity of the insights driving business decisions. Safeguarding this information is not just a technological concern but a fundamental aspect of ethical decision-making in the digital age.

Collaboration tools like Slack or Microsoft Teams are also changing the landscape of strategic decisions. By facilitating seamless communication and collaboration within and across teams, they ensure that valuable insights don't remain siloed. When teams can share ideas, discuss challenges, and collaborate in real-time, the collective intelligence of the organization is harnessed, leading to richer, more comprehensive decisions.

Lastly, the prospects of artificial intelligence in decision-making tools are both exciting and promising. As AI continues to evolve, its potential to aid strategic decisions broadens. Machine learning algorithms analyze data at unprecedented speeds, identifying patterns and anomalies with accuracy that challenges human limitations. These AI-driven insights can empower leaders to hone their strategies with a level of precision previously unattainable.

Despite the marvels of modern technology, the ultimate goal of these tools is to support human intelligence, not replace it. By embracing these technologies, leaders can enhance their ability to interpret data, visualize potential futures, and align their decisions with organizational values. Software and apps, when chosen and used wisely, become extensions of our decision-making capabilities—a powerful synergy between human insight and technological prowess.

Evaluating Technology's Impact

In today's fast-paced world, decision-making tools and technologies have become indispensable allies in navigating high-stakes scenarios. The integration of technology in decision-making processes offers profound advantages, yet it also presents challenges that must be carefully evaluated. This dual-edged nature of technology commands an understanding that goes beyond surface-level engagement to truly assess its impact.

Weighing the impact of technology begins with recognizing its capacity to transform data into actionable insights. Data analytics, artificial intelligence, and machine learning algorithms are revolutionizing the way information is processed, providing decision-makers with an unprecedented ability to forecast outcomes with greater accuracy. It's about harnessing the power of data to not just see what is, but to anticipate what will be. Embracing such capabilities can provide a strategic edge, yet it's crucial to remain mindful of the limitations inherent in any technological solution.

One of the significant advantages of technology is efficiency. Algorithms and software can process large datasets quickly, offering insights within moments that would take humans much longer to derive. This speed is crucial in high-pressure situations where time is often of the essence. But, efficiency shouldn't come at the expense of accuracy or depth of understanding. Technology can sometimes overlook the subtleties that human judgment considers, which means decision-makers need to balance automated insights with personal intuition and critical thinking.

However, there's more to evaluate beyond just raw data processing. Technology also plays an integral role in enhancing collaboration among decision-makers. Tools supporting real-time communication and coordination allow teams to integrate diverse perspectives swiftly, leading to more holistic decisions. The shift towards cloud-based platforms and collaborative software reduces geographical barriers and fosters a more inclusive decision-making environment. But we must remember: technology is only as effective as the people using it. It requires a cultural shift in how teams operate, highlighting the importance of training and effective communication.

Moreover, technology's capacity to democratize information represents another key impact area. By making information more accessible, technology empowers a broader spectrum of individuals to participate in the decision-making process. This democratization can lead to more innovative and comprehensive solutions as diverse viewpoints are considered. However, an abundance of information can lead to information overload, making it crucial for decision-makers to discern relevant data from noise.

In evaluating technology's impact, it is paramount to address the ethical concerns that arise with its use. As decision-making tools become more sophisticated, issues related to privacy, data security, and algorithmic bias become prominent. These concerns are not just technical challenges; they are deeply rooted in ethical considerations that shape the integrity and fairness of decision-making processes. Decision-makers must navigate these waters carefully, ensuring that the technology they rely on aligns with their organization's ethical standards and societal norms.

The advent of AI and machine learning comes with promises of precision and predictive power, yet these technologies often operate within black boxes. This lack of transparency can undermine confidence in automated decisions. Understanding and interpreting machine outputs require a new set of skills and a degree of technological literacy that decision-makers must develop. As technology continues to evolve, so too must the educational frameworks that prepare professionals for this new landscape.

While technology provides tools that enhance decision-making, it is vital to remember the human element that drives these tools. It is fundamentally people who interpret data, ask the right questions, and make the final decisions. Technology serves as an augmentative aid, not a replacement. Cultivating team members' decision-making skills remains as important as ever, ensuring they can effectively wield technological tools to complement their judgment.

Furthermore, the strategic deployment of technology can shape the way decisions are made at both operational and strategic levels. At an operational level, technology can streamline processes, reduce errors, and improve consistency. At a strategic level, it supports long-term planning and helps to identify future opportunities and threats. Decision-makers must evaluate which technologies are best suited for their specific needs, considering factors such as scalability, ease of integration, and long-term sustainability.

Reflecting on the impact of technology requires continuous adaptation. The landscape of decision-making technology is dynamic, with innovations emerging regularly. Staying informed about the latest developments enables decision-makers to adapt their strategies, ensuring they leverage cutting-edge tools that offer genuine value. This involves not just keeping pace with technological advancements but also anticipating how these changes will affect decision-making frameworks in the future.

Ultimately, evaluating technology's impact on decision-making is about finding balance. It's about leveraging technological strengths while acknowledging its limitations. It's about integrating technology into the decision-making fabric in a way that amplifies human capability rather than replacing it. By doing so, decision-makers will not only make more informed choices but also inspire a culture of innovation and ethical responsibility.

The path to mastering decision-making in the age of technology lies in a combination of embracing new tools and honing human judgment. Through an astute evaluation of technology's impact, professionals can better navigate complex landscapes, build robust decision-making models, and thrive in environments fraught with uncertainty. This approach ensures they're equipped to make decisions that are not just informed and timely but also aligned with broader organizational values and goals.

Chapter 18: Personalized Decision-Making Styles

Recognizing and embracing your unique decision-making style is like discovering a personal blueprint for navigating the complex landscape of high-stakes choices. Each decision-maker possesses distinct tendencies influenced by their personality, experiences, and values, which shape how they confront pressure and uncertainty. The key to leveraging your personalized style lies in identifying your strengths and areas for growth, thereby tailoring strategies that align with your natural inclinations. Whether you rely on analytical scrutiny, trust your instincts, or strike a balance between the two, honing this self-awareness empowers you to make decisive, confident, and effective decisions. By syncing your approach with your distinctive style, you not only enhance your ability to act under pressure but also inspire others to tap into their own personalized decision-making frameworks. Let your style guide you to not just respond to challenges, but to lead with clarity and resolve.

Identifying Your Decision-Making Type

Embarking on the journey of mastering decision-making under pressure requires an intimate understanding of one's own decision-making style. Each individual has a unique approach that is influenced by past experiences, innate tendencies, and personal preferences. Identifying your decision-making type is akin to holding a mirror up to your cognitive processes; it's about recognizing strengths you can harness and limitations you need to address. By becoming aware of how you make decisions, especially when stakes are high, you can refine your approach, supplement weaknesses, and leverage your natural strengths to their full potential.

To start figuring out your decision-making type, it can be helpful to reflect on how you typically make decisions at work or in high-pressure situations. Do you rely heavily on data, or do you prefer to go with your gut feelings? Are you someone who likes to deliberate extensively, or do you tend to make quick decisions? Understanding these tendencies lays the groundwork for enhancing your decision-making processes. Humans are complex, so it's common for one's decision-making style to incorporate a bit of everything—an analytical mind might also have strong intuitive insights, for instance.

Identifying your type involves a process of introspection, feedback, and often a bit of trial and error. You might begin by reflecting on past decisions. Consider a few instances where the pressure was high, and identify what influenced your choices. Were you driven more by logic or emotion? Did you seek out others' opinions, or did you rely solely on your judgment? Taking time to dissect your past decisions can reveal patterns in your decision-making behavior.

Moreover, ask for feedback from colleagues or peers—others can often see our patterns and tendencies more clearly than we do ourselves. They might point out instances where you've been particularly decisive or recall moments where your hesitation was palpable. This external perspective adds another layer of understanding to your self-assessment, offering insights you may overlook in your personal reflections.

Another avenue for exploring your decision-making type is through structured assessments or psychological tests. Tools like the Myers-Briggs Type Indicator or the Big Five personality traits can highlight aspects of your personality that influence decision-making, such as openness to experience or tolerance for ambiguity. While no test can define you entirely, they provide language and frameworks that can guide your exploration.

Once you've identified your basic tendencies, it's crucial to consider the context in which you're operating. What works in one environment or scenario might not be effective in another. For professionals in high-stakes environments, adaptability is key. Imagine a scenario where quick decisions are required but your style leans naturally toward thorough analysis. In such cases, you need strategies to speed up your decision-making process without compromising too much on accuracy.

In contrast, if your style is more intuitive, there may be instances when a more data-driven approach would yield better results. It's important to identify when to stick to your natural style and when to modify your approach in response to the demands of the situation. This adaptability in decision-making is what sets apart good leaders from great ones.

After identifying your decision-making type, the next step is to refine your skills in alignment with your personal style. This involves embracing lifelong learning and openness to new techniques. Personal and professional development practices can greatly enhance your decision-making effectiveness. Regularly exposing yourself to new challenges or deliberately putting yourself in decision-heavy scenarios can stretch your capabilities.

Building a support system also helps fortify your decision-making. Engaging with mentors, seeking input from diverse teams, and encouraging open dialogues can provide support and uncover blind spots you might have missed. It's about creating an environment that complements your decision-making style, ensuring that when pressure mounts, you're equipped and confident in your approach.

Finally, recognize that your decision-making type can evolve over time. As you grow and gather more experiences, you might find shifts in your preferences and abilities. Staying open to change and acknowledging this evolution connects deeply with personal growth. By staying aware of not just who you are now, but who you are becoming, your decision-making will remain dynamic, nuanced, and effective in any situation.

Tailoring Strategies to Fit Your Style

In the fast-paced rhythm of our professional lives, decision-making isn't just an isolated action; it's a dance of intuition, experience, and adaptation. Each person's path to reaching decisions bears a unique imprint, shaped by individual traits and circumstances. As professionals encountering high-stakes decisions, understanding how we make decisions and tailoring strategies to our distinct styles can empower us to thrive under pressure. But how do we uncover and leverage this personal style for effective decision-making?

First, begin by acknowledging that there is no one-size-fits-all model. Just as every leader from Machiavelli to modern executives has honed their strategies over time, we too must navigate a complex landscape of personal perception and situation-specific nuances. Identifying your decision-making type is crucial, which acts as a compass, directing us through the often intricate decision-making process. Are you more data-driven or do you lean on your gut feelings? Insights into your usual approach can shed light on what drives your choices and how you react under pressure.

For example, someone who relies heavily on analytical skills may benefit from reinforcing their data-oriented strategies with intuitive insights. On the other hand, if you tend to favor intuition, finding a balance with fact-based analysis can fill potential gaps in reasoning that raw instinct may overlook. Recognizing and embracing this duality, rather than focusing exclusively on one aspect, ensures a well-rounded perspective when making crucial decisions. Tailoring your approach involves integrating complementary techniques that support and challenge your preferred decision-making style, creating a rich tapestry of informed and intuitive choices.

Moreover, understanding your natural decision-making style can also influence how you process urgency and complexity. Some individuals thrive on making snap decisions in high-stakes scenarios, driven by adrenaline and instinct. For them, improving decision-making might involve learning to pause when necessary, ensuring that crucial details are not overlooked amidst the momentum. Meanwhile, those who deliberate extensively could benefit from practicing speed and assertiveness, fostering confidence in drawing swift conclusions when the situation demands.

Imagine you're preparing for a critical negotiation or planning a corporate strategy that could pivot your company's trajectory. In these moments, customizing your decision-making strategies requires a blend of self-awareness and agility. Think of it as curating a personal toolkit—equipping yourself with resources and techniques that resonate with your style while also preparing for unexpected challenges. Identifying the right tools is akin to a craftsman selecting the perfect instruments for a masterpiece; they enhance your natural skills and maximize your effectiveness.

Once you have a clear sense of your decision-making style, continuously test its limits. Seek feedback and refine your strategies through experiences that push boundaries. The crucible of high-stakes environments is both a challenge and an opportunity. Each decision you face under pressure offers a chance to evaluate what works and what doesn't. This reflective adaptation is key to not only improving your personal decision-making style but also to being resilient in the face of new challenges.

Consider adopting a mindset of playful experimentation. Allow yourself the flexibility to switch strategies in different contexts and reflect on the outcomes. For instance, you might try approaching a typically methodical decision with an intuitive angle, and vice versa. Discovering these nuances could be a revelation, signaling opportunities for growth and refinement within your existing framework.

Furthermore, engaging with peer networks and diverse teams can illuminate blind spots and enhance your perspective. Diversity in decision-making styles often brings fresh insights and challenges your assumptions. By observing and understanding how others approach decisions, you can incorporate elements that might have been absent in your own process, enriching your personal strategy.

The journey to tailoring your decision-making strategies is a dynamic, ongoing process. By tapping into your core style while remaining open to evolution, you prepare yourself not just for the decisions of today, but also for those of tomorrow. Embrace this opportunity, continuously shape your approach, and find empowerment knowing that each choice is a step towards mastery in your professional life. As you refine and deploy your bespoke decision-making toolkit, remember that the ability to lead effectively under pressure is not a destination but a constantly evolving journey.

Chapter 19: Decision-Making in Diverse Teams

In decision-making within diverse teams, the true strength lies not only in the variety of perspectives but in synthesizing these differences into innovative solutions. A mix of backgrounds, experiences, and viewpoints can fuel creativity and lead to more comprehensive decision outcomes. But this diversity can also present challenges, such as potential conflicts and misunderstandings. To navigate these complexities, leaders must cultivate an environment where differences are valued, and open dialogue is encouraged. By leaning into diversity, teams can unlock new pathways to decision-making, finding unique approaches to tackle even the most daunting challenges. It requires empathy, active listening, and an unwavering commitment to seeing conflicts not as barriers but as opportunities for deeper understanding and growth. As each voice finds its place, the collective wisdom expands, transforming high-stakes decisions into shared victories, with every team member invested in the outcome.

Harnessing the Power of Diversity

Imagine a kaleidoscope. Each twist or turn rearranges bright shards of glass into stunning patterns, unique and ever-changing. Similarly, diverse teams bring together a variety of perspectives, experiences, and insights, crafting solutions that a homogenous group might never discover. When it comes to decision-making, the metaphor isn't merely poetic; it's practical. Diverse teams hold an untapped reservoir of creativity, capable of dissolving even the most daunting challenges.

Let's delve into why diversity matters in decision-making. Consider this: every person carries a distinct cognitive toolkit—the culmination of upbringing, education, professional background, and life experiences. A group that harnesses this multitude of perspectives taps into cognitive diversity, generating a richer pool of ideas. Simply put, when team members approach a problem from different angles, they see facets others might miss, similar to how different lenses can change the view of a landscape.

Moreover, diverse teams often outperform homogeneous ones in problem-solving, but the reasons are rooted in deeper psychological benefits. Diversity reduces the occurrence of groupthink, a psychological phenomenon where the desire for harmony or conformity results in irrational or dysfunctional decision-making outcomes. By encouraging different viewpoints, diverse teams are better equipped to challenge assumptions and push the boundaries of conventional thinking. This dynamic isn't just theoretical—it's backed by research from leading institutions that demonstrate diversity's positive impact on innovation and performance.

But while diversity is a powerful asset, it requires conscious cultivation to flourish. Leaders must recognize the psychological safety necessary for team members to voice dissenting opinions without fear of repercussions. If individuals feel secure, they're more likely to share unique insights and take creative risks. A supportive environment where each member feels empowered to contribute nurtures not just participation but meaningful engagement.

A pertinent question emerges: How can teams actively harness the power of diversity? It starts with intentionality in team composition. When forming a team, consider the mix of demographics, skills, and experiences each member brings. But don't stop there. Nurture an inclusive culture by promoting open dialogue and encouraging a mindset of curiosity and learning. When employees feel valued for their diverse viewpoints, they become more engaged and invested in their team's success.

Moreover, successful teams often employ structured techniques to make the most of their diversity. For example, "devil's advocate" roles are effective in ensuring critical appraisal of ideas. Rotating this role among team members can democratize disagreements and further solidify trust. Another technique involves using diverse pilot teams for testing new initiatives, thus gaining a more comprehensive understanding of potential outcomes before full-scale implementation.

Communication in diverse teams also requires thoughtful strategies. While conflicting viewpoints can be enlightening, they can also lead to misunderstandings if communication is not clear and respectful. Encouraging active listening and empathetic conversations can bridge gaps and build stronger relationships. Simple practices like restating others' perspectives before responding foster better comprehension and a deeper appreciation for differing views.

Diversity extends beyond cultural and demographic variables. Diverse teams benefit also from variations in cognitive styles, educational backgrounds, and professional experiences. For instance, pairing analytical thinkers with creative ideators can result in solutions that are both innovative and practicable. In this way, diversity isn't a checkbox—it's a convergence of thoughts that propels the entire decision-making process forward.

Interestingly, research also highlights a curious phenomenon: diversity might initially slow down decision-making processes. The clash of viewpoints calls for more discussions and deliberations, but this 'slowness' should be reframed as a strength rather than a setback. The extra time spent in understanding different perspectives actually enriches the decision framework. It aligns with a mindset that values exhaustive consideration over rash conclusions.

The process of navigating diverse opinions sharpens a team's critical thinking skills. It's like a rigorous workout for the collective brain muscle, making it more adept at tackling future challenges. Decision-making becomes not just a task but a collaborative exercise, enhancing each member's skills and promoting a culture of ongoing learning and growth.

It's important to acknowledge that diversity can also bring conflicts, as varying viewpoints naturally lead to disagreements. However, it is the very process of resolving these conflicts that can enhance decision-making. Constructive conflict fosters an environment where team members critically analyze each other's reasoning, leading to more robust solutions. Leaders can guide this process by focusing on shared goals, ensuring that team members don't lose sight of their collective purpose.

Finally, let's remember that a diverse team is not an endpoint but a beginning. Teams must continuously work to maintain and empower their diversity. This includes revisiting team dynamics regularly and recalibrating strategies to adapt to new challenges. When diversity is leveraged effectively, it doesn't just improve decision-making in the present—it's a long-term investment in a team's capacity to adapt and innovate in the face of future challenges.

In summary, harnessing the power of diversity is not just about representation. It's about creating a vibrant ecosystem of voices, where every member's perspective builds towards better, more inclusive decision-making. As we move forward, let diversity be our compass, guiding teams to uncharted terrains of creativity and achievement, proving that together, we're capable of more than we could ever accomplish alone.

Resolving Conflicts in Group Decisions

Decision-making in diverse teams is as much about embracing different perspectives as it is about managing the inevitable conflicts that arise from them. In environments where diversity thrives, so too does tension, driven by contrasting viewpoints, cultural differences, and varied problem-solving methodologies. Yet, it is precisely these divergent points of view that can lead to groundbreaking solutions, if navigated effectively. The challenge, then, lies in turning potential discord into constructive dialogue and mutual understanding.

The first step toward resolving conflicts in group decisions is recognizing the value of every team member's perspective. Each participant brings unique insights, shaped by their backgrounds and experiences, enriching the team's collective intelligence. Successful teams understand that disagreement is not only natural but necessary for innovation. They create spaces where team members feel empowered to voice dissenting opinions without fear of retribution or marginalization.

For conflicts to be resolved, communication must be prioritized, and its flow within the team needs to be transparent and equitable. Effective communication is not just about speaking but actively listening. This involves listening to understand, not just to reply, and ensuring that everyone gets the opportunity to contribute. Techniques like active listening and reflective questioning can help bring hidden concerns to the surface and clarify misunderstandings. Remember, the goal is to reach a shared understanding, not necessarily a unanimous agreement.

Conflicts can escalate when emotions run high, so cultivating emotional intelligence within the team is crucial. Being aware of one's emotions and those of others can prevent misunderstandings and help de-escalate tensions. Teams that develop the ability to acknowledge and manage emotions are more likely to find creative solutions to problems. This emotional competence fosters a supportive group dynamic, turning potential conflict from a source of division into an opportunity for connection and growth.

Setting clear goals and expectations is another powerful tool in conflict resolution. When team members are aligned on the objectives and the criteria for success, decisions become more focused and less contentious. Clear expectations provide a roadmap, helping teams to evaluate decisions based on how well they align with established goals. This alignment requires regular check-ins and updates to ensure everyone remains on the same path, reducing the likelihood of misunderstandings and conflicting agendas.

Facilitating decision-making sessions with structure and purpose can transform conflicts into productive outcomes. This involves setting agendas, defining roles, and agreeing on decision-making processes beforehand. Utilizing methods like the Six Thinking Hats or the Delphi Technique can guide discussions, helping to manage conflicts by systematically addressing all aspects of a problem. These structured approaches ensure that every viewpoint is considered, promoting fairness and reducing bias.

Moreover, it is essential to recognize when consensus is not achievable and to be comfortable with compromise or 'agreeing to disagree.' Not every conflict will have a clear resolution, and that's okay. Leaders should foster an environment where team members feel safe to express differing opinions and can move forward with decisions even when there isn't complete consensus. Emphasizing that diversity of thought is an asset, not a setback, can lead to innovative approaches that might never have been considered in a more homogeneous setting.

In situations where conflicts persist or escalate, mediators or neutral third parties can be invaluable. These individuals can provide an unbiased perspective, helping teams to navigate emotionally charged discussions and find common ground. Mediation can help clarify misunderstandings, diffuse tension, and facilitate a resolution that respects the interests of all parties involved.

In the context of diverse teams, embracing cultural competence is critical. Understanding and respecting cultural differences can prevent misinterpretations and foster a more inclusive decision-making environment. Team members should be encouraged to share their cultural norms and communication styles, enriching the team's collective understanding and ability to engage constructively.

Ultimately, the goal is not simply to resolve conflicts but to learn and grow from them. Teams that engage in reflection and feedback processes are better equipped to handle future conflicts. After decisions are made, teams should evaluate the decision-making process, identifying what worked well and what can be improved. This practice of continuous learning cultivates a culture of openness and adaptability, which is essential in high-pressure decision-making scenarios.

Empowerment plays a significant role in conflict resolution. When individuals feel valued and empowered within a team, they are more likely to engage constructively in conflict resolution and decision-making processes. Empowerment comes from trust, and trusting teams are more resilient in the face of conflict. Leaders should focus on building this trust by encouraging open dialogue, showing appreciation for contributions, and recognizing the strengths each team member brings to the table.

By reorienting our view of conflict as an integral part of decision-making in diverse teams, we can unlock the creative potential inherent in these differences. Conflicts, when managed well, don't just end; they transform, guiding teams toward innovative solutions that reflect a wide range of perspectives. In high-pressure environments where decisions can have far-reaching consequences, the ability to navigate and resolve conflicts is not just beneficial—it is essential.

Chapter 20: Preparing for the Unpredictable

In the ever-evolving world of high-stakes decision-making, the ability to prepare for the unpredictable becomes not just advantageous but essential. Consider this: life's uncertainties don't ask for permission or wait for us to catch up. To thrive amidst volatility, it is crucial to develop robust scenario planning techniques and adaptive strategies. This chapter explores how professionals like yourself can embrace uncertainty with creativity and foresight, transforming potential chaos into opportunities for success. By crafting a toolkit that combines strategic foresight with agile responses, you'll not only prepare for unexpected challenges but also enhance your confidence in navigating uncharted waters. Whether you're leading a team facing industry disruptions or making split-second decisions that impact your organization, the techniques and mindset presented here are designed to empower you to step forward fearlessly, ready to capitalize on whatever comes next.

Scenario Planning Techniques

Imagine a pilot preparing for a flight. Before take-off, they're not just planning for clear skies and smooth air currents. They also consider various scenarios—from engine failures to severe weather disturbances. This process of thinking ahead, of envisioning different futures, is called scenario planning. It's a technique that has proven essential for professionals who must navigate the unpredictable, a skill that is more art than science.

Unlike other strategies that may rely heavily on exact predictions, scenario planning involves crafting multiple potential futures based on different variables that could influence decision outcomes. It doesn't seek to forecast one definite future but prepares you for any number of possibilities. By identifying key uncertainties and forces that could affect your decisions, you open yourself up to a spectrum of pathways. You become more agile, more equipped to respond rather than react.

At its core, scenario planning juxtaposes imagination with rigorous analysis. It invites you to ask, "What if?" and to explore those questions deeply. This requires a balance between creativity and critical thinking—a dance between envisioning different worlds and preparing to operate within them. As one examines each scenario, the objective is not to predict the future but to explore it. This exploration enables you to recognize opportunities that may otherwise remain hidden.

This technique has roots dating back to the military and megacorporations, where the stakes of being unprepared are exceptionally high. For example, energy companies have long used it to plan for shifts in market forces and regulatory changes. By considering what could happen if oil prices doubled or new environmental policies emerged, they develop strategies that can weather various environmental, economic, or geopolitical changes. What can professionals learn from this? The crucial lesson is about the value of anticipation and flexibility.

Begin by defining the scope. What are the key decisions or questions that need exploration? Pinpoint the driving forces—those critical elements in your environment that could shape outcomes. These might include technological advancements, market trends, regulatory shifts, or even sociopolitical dynamics. Consider both the predictable and those elements that lie beyond current understanding. Create a framework for thinking broadly about the environment in which decisions will unfold.

Once identified, organize these forces into certain and uncertain factors. Certainties—like demographic trends—are straightforward. They can be plotted with reasonable accuracy. Uncertainties, however, are where scenario planning breathes life. These are the wild cards. Think about potential disruptions, novel competitors, emerging technologies, or changes in consumer behavior. What if a new technology renders your current business model obsolete? How would you adapt or pivot? This categorization allows you to better anticipate and build resilience against different eventualities.

Developing detailed and diverse scenarios comes next. Let's say you're exploring scenarios around a business expansion decision. One scenario might involve successful market entry with economic growth; another could illustrate a scenario where a competitor beats you with innovative tech. Creating three to four distinctive scenarios is often recommended. More than four, and the analysis might become unmanageable; fewer, and you risk overlooking critical alternatives.

In these narratives, the aim is to paint a vivid picture of the future. What do customers want? What technologies flourish? What regulations challenge or support your operations? Engage other stakeholders in this process—different perspectives provide a richer, more nuanced understanding of potential futures, reinforcing the idea that impactful decisions rarely occur in a vacuum.

With detailed scenarios at hand, evaluate your strategies. How does each scenario impact your plans? Are there common responses that can be cross-applied, regardless of which scenario might unfold? This synthesis not only reveals robust strategies but also highlights vulnerabilities within your current plan. It reveals areas where you need to build capabilities or hedge against risk. Don't think of these scenarios as static documents. They're dynamic guides meant to evolve as new information arises.

Moreover, consider embedding these scenarios into simulations or role-plays. Test your responses to each potential future as if you're rehearsing a play. This brings a theoretical exercise into reality, giving you and your team practical insights about adaptability and readiness. Leaders will find that these trials encourage better, more resilient decision-making by providing a rehearsal space without the pressures of real-world consequences.

Lastly, integrate what you've learned back into your strategic planning process. Scenario planning should not be an isolated exercise; it should be interwoven with your organization's regular planning cycles. By doing so, you ensure that your strategies remain relevant in a fast-evolving world. This ongoing recalibration allows you to remain aligned with market demands and ready to capitalize on unexpected opportunities.

In the grand tapestry of high-stakes decision-making, scenario planning functions as both a compass and a map. It doesn't eliminate uncertainty but provides the tools to navigate it confidently. As you cultivate these skills, you create a future that draws heavily on anticipation rather than reaction—allowing not just survival but flourishment in times of unpredictability.

Adaptive Strategies for Changing Conditions

In a world characterized by volatility, uncertainty lingers as a constant. For professionals tasked with making high-stakes decisions, it becomes imperative to harness adaptive strategies to navigate shifting landscapes effectively. An adaptive strategy is not just a safety net; it's an integral compass for any decision-maker charting through unknown waters.

One of the foundational aspects of developing adaptive strategies is cultivating an agile mindset. Flexibility isn't merely a desirable trait but a crucial skill. Decision-makers need to pivot quickly when confronting unforeseen obstacles. This form of agility enables leaders to respond dynamically rather than reactively, maintaining poise and direction.

A practical approach to agility is scenario planning. By envisioning possible futures, decision-makers can anticipate various outcomes and prepare actionable responses. Whether the situation involves sudden market shifts or unexpected regulatory changes, having rehearsed potential scenarios enables quicker and more precise decision-making.

Scenario planning involves visualizing best-case, worst-case, and most likely scenarios. In doing so, professionals arm themselves with a repertoire of possible responses. The key here isn't predicting the future with certainty but reducing the element of surprise and enhancing readiness.

However, mere visualization doesn't suffice. Maintenance of a feedback loop is essential. Decision-makers should seek insights from stakeholders and team members regularly, as this provides diverse perspectives. Creating environments that encourage open dialogue fortifies adaptive strategies, refining them through collaborative input.

Consider the interdependence of intuition and analysis as a dual-axis approach to adaptation. Leveraging data is crucial, yet intuition honed by experience can illuminate paths that numbers might overlook. Combining these elements forms a robust decision-making structure that adapts to evolving conditions without faltering.

Moreover, adaptive strategies require continual learning and reflection. Reflection acts as a barometer, measuring the adequacy of responses to past challenges. By continuously dissecting successes and failures, decision-makers refine their strategies in anticipation of future challenges.

Integrating new technologies can bolster adaptive strategies significantly. Technology offers tools for real-time data analytics, enhancing the capability to adapt swiftly. Rapid access to significant data enables decision-makers to align strategies promptly with prevailing conditions.

Yet, with the ubiquity of technology comes its own set of challenges. Decision-makers must discern which technologies enhance adaptability and which could potentially complicate decision-making processes. Evaluation and selective adoption of technology are crucial components of effective strategy development.

Empathy, although often underestimated, plays an essential role in adaptability. Understanding team members' needs and incentivizing participation in decision-making processes fortifies engagement and versatility. Empathetic leadership can elicit proactive contributions from the team during unpredictable times.

Furthermore, resilience is the cornerstone of adaptive strategic management. Building resilience equips teams to withstand shocks and recover swiftly, minimizing operational disruptions. Resilience isn't about avoiding challenges, but rather enduring and learning from them to strengthen future responses. Cultivating resilience within teams ensures steadfastness in the face of unpredictability.

Another pivotal element in developing adaptive strategies is the alignment of core values with strategic objectives. By anchoring strategies in clearly defined principles, decision-makers ensure consistency, even as immediate tactics might shift in response to change. When core values are clear, adaptations still reflect the organization's vision and mission.

Ultimately, decision-makers must embrace the inevitability of change. Transitioning mindset from a static to a dynamic perception of the environment is key. This acceptance transcends beyond merely surviving the pressures of unpredictability; it involves thriving within those parameters by viewing change as an opportunity for growth.

By incorporating adaptive strategies, professionals not only prepare for the unpredictable but also transform potential challenges into strategic advantages. In doing so, they cultivate an environment where change fuels innovation and progress rather than hindrance. This approach not only maximizes resilience but also strategically positions organizations to excel in an ever-evolving landscape.

Chapter 21: Accountability and Decision Ownership

In the high-stakes arena of professional decision-making, embracing accountability and owning one's choices are paramount. Every decision, whether triumphant or flawed, casts a ripple of consequences that affects not just the decision-maker but also those around them. It's about taking responsibility, not only for the outcomes but also for the process itself. When professionals understand the weight of their choices, they foster a culture where transparency becomes a core ethic. From this foundation, trust is built and sustained, empowering teams to act decisively and with confidence. In cultivating such an environment, leaders also inspire others to recognize their role in every decision, transforming challenges into opportunities for growth and innovation. True accountability is not a burden but a catalyst for driving meaningful change and exemplary leadership in any organization.

Understanding the Consequences of Choices

The decisions we make, particularly in high-pressure contexts, ripple outward in ways that can be surprisingly profound. This isn't just about the immediate effects of a choice, but also the secondary and tertiary impacts that can unfold over time. Understanding these outcomes is crucial for professionals looking to refine their decision-making capabilities. In fact, acknowledging the weight of one's choices is the first step toward embracing accountability and decision ownership, a core tenet of leadership.

Consider the interconnected nature of today's professional environments. A decision made in haste, without fully considering potential consequences, can easily lead to cascading effects throughout an organization. It might start with a minor misstep, like choosing a less effective supplier to save costs, only to later realize the supplier can't meet demand, leading to production delays and customer dissatisfaction. The capacity to anticipate such outcomes depends largely on an individual's ability to pause, reflect, and project beyond the immediate.

The art of forecasting the consequences of choices relies heavily on experience, but experience alone isn't enough. It also requires a deep understanding of the context and stakeholders involved. When faced with a decision, it's beneficial to ask: *If this scenario unfolds as planned, who benefits? Who suffers? What resources are affected?* By methodically evaluating these questions, we begin to paint a more holistic picture of the possible trajectories stemming from our decisions.

Moreover, understanding the consequences of our choices also helps us mitigate risks. By anticipating potential outcomes, we can develop contingency plans that allow for adaptive responses rather than reactive ones. This proactive mindset fosters resilience and strategic adaptability, enabling leaders to manage crises efficiently. As noted by many successful leaders, the ability to adapt swiftly is often a bigger asset than sticking rigidly to a single, predetermined course of action.

Yet, seeing the full scope of a decision's consequences isn't solely about identifying risks. It's also about recognizing opportunities. A choice might unlock avenues for growth, development, and innovation that weren't initially apparent. By training ourselves to view decision-making through the lens of possibility, we can harness the latent potential within every option. A simple shift in perspective can transform decision-making from a daunting challenge into an exciting exploration of future potential.

Nonetheless, it's important to acknowledge that we'll inevitably encounter unintended consequences. Even the most meticulously considered decision can yield surprises. The key here is not to fear them but to learn from them. An effective decision-maker acknowledges mistakes, drawing lessons from them to improve future decisions. This iterative process not only sharpens decision-making skills but also enriches an organizational culture with insights drawn from real-world experience.

Furthermore, accountability becomes a driving force in understanding the consequences of choices. When decision-makers take ownership of their decisions—and the resulting outcomes—they cultivate trust both personally and within their teams. Such trust is foundational for collaboration, a critical element in any high-stakes environment. Transparency in decision-making fosters a sense of shared purpose, encouraging team members to engage more closely with organizational goals and to contribute their own insights and expertise.

However, embracing accountability is easier said than done. It demands courage and humility. It requires us to confront our errors without deflection and to make amends when needed. Simultaneously, it calls for the conviction to stand by sound decisions, even when outcomes deviate from expectations. This dynamic interplay between ownership and humility cultivates credibility, a crucial trait for any leader.

In parallel, leaders should strive to instill a culture where consequences of decisions are openly discussed and analyzed. Such openness encourages an atmosphere of continuous learning and improvement. By regularly reflecting on outcomes, both successful and otherwise, organizations can build a repository of insights that guide future decision-making processes. This not only enhances individual competence but also strengthens the collective prowess of the team.

Encouraging dialogue about decisions and their impacts also emboldens team members to voice dissenting perspectives, nurture innovative solutions, and embrace diverse thinking paths. Diverse opinions can reveal insights that might not surface in homogenous groups, often leading to more rounded and effective decisions. Therefore, harnessing the strengths of a diverse and inclusive team can be a significant asset in navigating the complexities of choice.

Essentially, understanding the consequences of choices is about fostering a mindset of responsibility and foresight. By examining every potential path a decision might take, weighing the benefits and drawbacks, and remaining vigilant of its unfolding consequences, we equip ourselves with the tools necessary for impactful leadership. This mindset positions us not only to respond to immediate pressures but to navigate the complex landscapes of tomorrow with agility and confidence.

Fostering a Culture of Accountability

In the realm of high-stakes decision-making, fostering a culture of accountability isn't just a best practice; it's essential. When individuals and teams take ownership of their decisions, the entire organization benefits. Accountability builds trust and encourages a proactive approach toward continuous improvement. It creates a transparent environment where mistakes are seen as learning opportunities rather than reasons for blame. But how do we cultivate such a culture effectively? It's a question worth exploring in any domain where decisions can have significant consequences.

Accountability begins with clearly defining roles and responsibilities. Everyone involved in the decision-making process must understand their role and the expectations that come with it. This clarity lays the foundation for a sense of ownership. When people know what's expected, they're more likely to take responsibility for their actions and the outcomes of their decisions. Moreover, clearly defined roles avoid confusion and overlap, allowing each team member to focus on their specific contributions without unintended interference.

Another key element in fostering accountability is establishing a feedback-rich environment. Feedback should be regular, constructive, and bi-directional. It's not just about leaders providing feedback to their teams, but also encouraging team members to voice their thoughts and reflections. This open communication loop ensures everyone stays aligned with the organization's goals and drives better outcomes. Feedback should not be limited to performance reviews; it must be integrated into the daily workflow, serving as a continuous loop for improvement.

Accountability thrives in an environment where failures are dissected, not punished. Leaders should encourage their teams to lean into challenges, take calculated risks, and learn from their setbacks. In a culture that sees mistakes as a natural part of the learning process, individuals are less afraid to take initiative. They come to see accountability not as a burden but as a chance to grow, innovate, and enhance their decision-making skills.

Encourage a shared vision among your team members to further embed accountability. When everyone is working towards common objectives, it becomes easier to align personal accountability with team and organizational goals. Shared vision promotes collective ownership, where successes are celebrated as a team, and failures are owned by everyone, not just the individual. This collective mindset often leads to higher motivation and commitment to achieving desired outcomes.

Transparency and openness play significant roles in cultivating a culture of accountability. When leaders communicate openly about decisions, processes, and outcomes, it demystifies the organizational trajectory and strengthens trust. Trust is the cornerstone of accountability. Team members who trust their leaders and peers are more likely to take responsibility because they feel supported. Trust, when paired with accountability, fosters a resilient and adaptive team capable of navigating high-pressure situations with confidence.

Accountability also demands personal commitment from each team member. It's about owning not just successes, but also recognizing areas for improvement and taking steps toward bettering one's skills. In high-stakes environments, personal development plans can serve as a roadmap for individuals, helping them align their goals with the organization's vision and thereby increasing their sense of accountability.

Leaders play a pivotal role in modeling accountability. Their behavior sets the tone for the entire team. When leaders admit their mistakes and learn from them, it signals that accountability isn't about punishment but about growth. This kind of leadership creates a safe space for team members to take ownership of their decisions, fostering an atmosphere where accountability is ingrained in the cultural fabric.

Moreover, establishing metrics and evaluation processes can reinforce accountability. By defining clear outcomes and benchmarks for success, organizations provide a tangible framework for assessing accountability. Regular assessments against these benchmarks help ensure that individuals and teams are taking responsible actions aligned with strategic goals.

Finally, it's crucial to recognize and reward accountable behavior. Celebrating those who embody accountability reinforces its importance and encourages others to mirror such behavior. Recognition doesn't always have to be grand; even simple acknowledgments of effort and commitment can nurture a culture where accountability flourishes.

Fostering a culture of accountability is no small feat, but its rewards are substantial. From bolstering trust to enhancing decision-making processes, the impacts of a well-cultivated culture are far-reaching. It empowers individuals and teams to approach decisions with clarity, courage, and commitment, ultimately leading to better outcomes in even the most high-pressure scenarios. By actively fostering accountability, organizations can build resilient teams prepared to tackle the challenges of today and the uncertainties of tomorrow.

Chapter 22: Long-Term Thinking in High-Stakes Decisions

When you're faced with high-stakes decisions, it's easy to get caught up in the urgency of the moment and overlook the broader implications of your choices. Long-term thinking requires a delicate balance between addressing immediate pressures and considering future goals. To cultivate a strategic vision, start by clearly defining what you ultimately want to achieve and how today's decisions could pave the path toward those aspirations. It's about understanding that short-term gains shouldn't come at the cost of long-term success. Successful decision-makers often employ strategic visioning techniques, which enable them to foresee potential scenarios and align their choices with their overarching mission. By adopting this mindset, you empower yourself not only to navigate the complexities of today's challenges but also to guide your team and organization toward sustainable growth and success. The ability to think long-term doesn't just affect the end result—it transforms the journey, fostering resilience and foresight that become invaluable in times of uncertainty.

Balancing Immediate Results with Future Goals

In the realm of high-stakes decision-making, the tension between immediate gratification and long-term success often dictates the path we choose. When pressure mounts, it's tempting to chase quick wins that promise instant relief or recognition. Yet, those who consistently excel in decision-making understand the importance of aligning immediate actions with broader, future-oriented goals. This section explores how professionals can navigate this delicate balance, ensuring their decisions not only handle the momentous challenges they face but also pave the way for sustainable success.

The first step in balancing immediate results with future goals is recognizing the broader context in which decisions are made. High-stakes situations, by their nature, often present dilemmas where short-term pressures clash with long-term visions. Leaders need to cultivate the ability to zoom out and view the current decision in the context of their ultimate objectives. They must resist the allure of choices that simply offer a quick fix, and instead, evaluate how such choices align with their strategic vision. This requires patience, foresight, and often, a degree of restraint.

Consider a business leader faced with a financial shortfall. The immediate instinct might be to initiate a widespread cost-cutting measure. And while this might stabilize the company in the short term, it could hinder innovation, employee morale, and the company's competitive edge in the future. A more balanced approach would involve identifying core areas essential for future growth and protecting those while finding efficiencies elsewhere. This way, acute problems are addressed without compromising long-term aspirations.

Successful long-term thinkers also recognize the importance of prioritizing. Not every urgent matter is equally consequential. The ability to distinguish between what's truly critical and what merely appears urgent can prevent leaders from being overwhelmed by the demands of the moment. It's here that the Eisenhower Matrix—a time management framework that helps prioritize tasks by urgency and importance—can be invaluable. By placing decisions within this matrix, leaders can maintain focus on long-term objectives while addressing immediate needs.

Communication plays a crucial role in reconciling short-term actions with long-term goals. Transparent communication ensures that everyone involved understands the rationale behind decisions, aligning their efforts toward a shared vision. Explaining how immediate tasks contribute to future success not only builds trust but also empowers team members to contribute more effectively. After all, a well-informed team is more likely to make decisions that are consistent with the organization's core values and strategic ambitions.

Moreover, integrating flexibility into decision-making processes can help keep long-term goals within reach, even when urgent issues arise. Leaders who are open to adaptation can pivot more easily when an immediate decision starts to veer away from achieving broader objectives. Flexibility doesn't mean having a loose commitment to goals; rather, it's about being agile enough to adjust tactics while keeping the end vision in sight. Such adaptability ensures that short-term decisions don't derail longer-term aspirations.

However, achieving this balance is no easy feat. It requires a mindset shift where long-term thinking is embedded into the cultural DNA of an organization or team. This involves continuously reinforcing the value of long-run planning during meetings, strategy sessions, and everyday interactions. By doing so, leaders embed a mental model whereby every decision, no matter how pressing, is seen through the lens of future impact. This paradigm shift ensures the team isn't swayed by transient wins but remains anchored in a forward-thinking approach.

Feedback loops are another invaluable tool for maintaining equilibrium between immediate and future-oriented decision-making. Implementing a system where decisions are revisited and outcomes are analyzed helps refine future choices. Leaders who encourage constructive feedback and learning from each decision build a culture that inherently balances immediate needs with long-term considerations. This reflective practice allows teams to recalibrate strategies as needed, improving both present-day decisions and future outcomes.

Ultimately, balancing short-term results with enduring goals is an ongoing challenge. It requires discipline, strategic thinking, and a willingness to look beyond the immediate horizon. Professionals who master this balance become adept at steering their decisions in a way that addresses present challenges while keeping their long-term vision intact. By integrating foresight with flexibility and fostering a mindset that prioritizes the future, leaders can navigate high-stakes scenarios with greater poise and confidence.

It's by embracing this holistic approach to decision-making that enduring success is built—not through isolated short-term victories, but through a sustained commitment to future goals. In doing so, decision-makers not only advance personally but elevate the potential of those around them, creating a legacy of thoughtful and impactful choices.

Strategic Visioning Techniques

Strategic visioning is an essential tool in the decision-making arsenal of any professional dealing with high-stakes scenarios. It allows leaders to chart a course through uncertainty with a clear view of desired outcomes. By honing the skill of strategic visioning, individuals can transcend the immediate pressure and navigate toward a better, more informed future. This section delves into practical techniques to harness strategic visioning effectively, promoting decisions that not only solve urgent problems but also align with long-term goals.

At its core, strategic visioning involves picturing a future so that decision-makers can lay down a path to achieve that future state. It's about converting an aspirational scenario into actionable steps. To start, it's essential to set a clear vision. This vision should act as a guiding star, something that inspires and motivates, but is also realistic and attainable. Unlike a simple goal, a vision provides a broader context and conveys the "why" behind decisions, thereby offering a sense of purpose.

Creating a strategic vision begins with introspection. Leaders should assess their values and priorities and reflect on what truly matters to them and their organization. This foundational work ensures that their vision is genuine and aligned with their core values. Visioning isn't just about individual aspirations; it involves understanding the values and objectives of the broader organization and its stakeholders. A well-rounded perspective helps create visions that capture the diverse needs and motivations of all involved, fostering a more cohesive and committed pursuit.

Once a vision is in place, breaking it down into medium- and short-term objectives is crucial. This layering approach helps maintain momentum and motivation, allowing for checkpoints that ensure you're on track to achieving the long-term vision. By identifying critical milestones and setting measurable targets, individuals can maintain focus without feeling overwhelmed by the enormity of the end goal.

Scenario planning is another powerful component of strategic visioning. It equips decision-makers to anticipate possible futures and adapt accordingly. It's not about predicting the future with certainty, but rather preparing for a range of possible outcomes. During this process, consider various internal and external factors that could impact your vision. Identifying potential challenges early allows for developing contingency plans that enhance resilience against unforeseen events.

Engaging with others during the strategic visioning process can offer fresh perspectives and uncover blind spots. By encouraging diverse viewpoints, leaders can anticipate potential pitfalls and enrich their vision with innovative ideas that might not have emerged from a singular perspective. Collaborative visioning ensures that any path forward is grounded in a shared reality, increasing buy-in and cooperation when it's time to act.

It's essential to acknowledge that uncertainty is a constant companion in any high-stakes decision. Embracing uncertainty involves not just preparing for the unknown with scenario planning, but also fostering a mindset that views it as an opportunity rather than a hindrance. Cultivating this mindset can lead to more innovative and creative solutions as you become more adaptive and responsive to change.

Once the strategic vision is articulated and the plan is charted, communicating it effectively is key. The ability to convey your vision clearly and compellingly can inspire and mobilize teams. When people understand and believe in the vision, they're more likely to commit to the efforts required to see it realized. Here, communication is not a one-way street; it's vital to encourage ongoing dialogue for feedback, ensuring that the vision evolves as necessary.

Maintaining flexibility is crucial. While it's important to be committed to your vision, being overly rigid can result in missed opportunities or an inability to pivot in the face of new evidence or changing circumstances. Regularly revisiting and revising your vision keeps it relevant and dynamic, ensuring that it remains aligned with current realities and future possibilities.

To bolster strategic visioning, adopting a reflective practice is beneficial. This involves regularly evaluating progress, understanding what strategies are working, and where adjustments are needed. Reflection not only ensures that actions remain aligned with the overarching vision but also facilitates continuous learning and improvement, hallmarks of effective long-term thinking.

Ultimately, strategic visioning is a powerful technique that transforms grand ambitions into achievable pathways through informed decision-making. By synthesizing long-term goals with daily actions, professionals can navigate high-stakes environments more confidently. As you refine these techniques, remember that visioning is as much an art as it is a science, requiring creativity, discipline, and a willingness to adapt. With practice, strategic visioning becomes an invaluable tool that empowers leaders to take control of their futures in an ever-changing world.

Chapter 23: Learning from Other Professions

Exploring decision-making strategies employed by other professions reveals valuable insights that transcend traditional boundaries and enrich our own approaches. Emergency services, for instance, operate under intense pressure, employing rapid evaluation and decisive action to save lives. Their ability to make swift, life-or-death decisions informs how we might handle high-stakes moments—by blending instinct with honed expertise. Meanwhile, the creative industries offer lessons in flexibility and innovation, demonstrating how embracing ambiguity and fostering creativity can lead to breakthroughs in critical situations. By learning from this diverse tapestry of professional experiences, we can cultivate a more adaptable, resilient decision-making style, one that thrives under pressure and uncertainty, turning challenges into opportunities for growth and success.

Emergency Services Decision-Making Models

When lives hang in the balance, the pressure to make quick, accurate decisions can be overwhelming. In the world of emergency services, professionals like firefighters, paramedics, and police officers face these intense situations daily. Their ability to succeed under such conditions offers valuable lessons for anyone eager to enhance decision-making skills in high-stakes environments. To draw from these experts, we must first understand how they've constructed models specifically designed to handle crises effectively.

The backbone of emergency decision-making models lies in protocol and training, honed through years of experience and analysis of real-life situations. Typically, these professionals start with rigorous training that prepares them for a variety of crisis scenarios. They practice with simulation models, which mimic emergency conditions, helping them build a repertoire of responses. Such preparation enables them to rely on muscle memory and instinct when real-life challenges arise. It's not so much that they react without thinking, rather, their thinking has become second nature. This level of preparedness is a cornerstone of their decision-making prowess.

A defining feature of these models is the ability to remain calm under pressure. Combatting anxiety and staying focused is critical when the stakes are high. Emergency services personnel are trained to maintain clarity by using techniques like controlled breathing and mental visualization. These practices help slow the body's stress response, allowing a clearer headspace for making decisions. For professionals in other fields seeking similar poise, incorporating these calming techniques into daily routines can be incredibly beneficial.

Equally important is adaptability. Situations in emergency settings can change rapidly, requiring swift adjustments to initial plans. Decision-making models in these services incorporate flexibility as a primary component. Personnel are often trained to reevaluate scenarios as new information comes in, ensuring that their responses are both timely and appropriate. The capacity to pivot and adapt strategies in real-time is a valuable skill set that transcends emergency services, offering critical insights for anyone whose decisions impact diverse scenarios.

Another key element is teamwork and communication. Emergency response teams rely heavily on each other for support and information. The ability to communicate clearly and effectively, even with competing noises and chaos, is indispensable. Roles within teams are clearly defined, ensuring everyone knows their responsibilities while having the freedom to make suggestions or reassess strategies as needed. Trust within teams accelerates the decision-making process, allowing for quick and confident responses. This aspect of shared responsibility can greatly enhance team dynamics in any field, fostering a more cohesive approach to problem-solving.

The use of technology and tools aids significantly in emergency services decision-making. Whether through sophisticated communication devices or life-saving equipment, technology serves as both a source of information and a means to execute decisions swiftly. Staying informed about the latest advancements and tools available in one's own field can offer similar benefits, providing a tactical advantage in critical moments.

Training doesn't just stop with technical skills. Emotional intelligence and empathy play essential roles too. Emergency professionals often face emotionally charged situations where personal interactions can have profound effects on outcomes. Developing a strong sense of empathy helps in understanding the stakes from every angle, be it for victims or colleagues. By using emotional intelligence cues, they enhance their ability to navigate complex human dynamics, ensure collaborative efforts, and foster a supportive environment that guides better decision-making.

After-action reviews are another cornerstone of these models. Post-crisis analysis helps emergency teams learn from their experiences, identify what went well, and highlight areas requiring improvement. This iterative process of feedback and adjustment cements their knowledge and skills, enabling continuous improvement. By adopting a similar mindset, professionals can leverage past experiences to drive future success, ensuring that each decision made contributes to personal and professional growth.

At the heart of emergency decision-making models is a foundation of ethics and values. Decisions are grounded in the core mission of protecting and saving lives, providing a guiding compass whenever tough choices arise. By clearly defining and internalizing one's values, individuals can make decisions that align with their broader goals, even in the face of pressure. Such alignment not only enhances the decision-making process but also helps in navigating moral complexities with confidence.

In looking to emergency services as a guide, it's clear that their structured yet flexible approach, rooted in preparation, adaptability, teamwork, and ethics, can be powerful when adapted to various high-stakes environments. By embracing these principles, along with strategies for maintaining calm and focusing on after-action improvements, decision-makers from any profession can cultivate the skills necessary to succeed when the pressure mounts. Learning from these seasoned professionals offers a reminder that, although decisions in crisis moments can seem daunting, with the right mindset and preparation, exceptional outcomes are not only possible but achievable.

Techniques from Creative Industries

Creative industries hold a unique position when it comes to decision-making under pressure. By their nature, fields such as film, music, fashion, and art are fueled by innovation, requiring quick thinking and adaptability. These industries thrive on high stakes, often making decisions that can lead to groundbreaking successes or dismal failures. Understanding their decision-making processes can offer valuable insights for anyone looking to improve their ability to make confident choices in high-pressure scenarios.

The creative process is inherently iterative. Artists, designers, and directors are familiar with the necessity of trial and error. They understand that initial ideas rarely end up in the final product. Instead, they embrace a cycle of creation, evaluation, and revision. This iterative approach is crucial in high-stakes decision-making. It teaches us that making a flawed decision initially isn't the end of the world. It's about having the courage to pivot, to critique constructively, and to adjust the course as necessary. Just like a film director who constantly reviews and alters scenes until they align perfectly with their vision, professionals can adopt this technique to refine their decision-making in real-time.

Moreover, collaboration in the creative industries is not just encouraged; it's vital. Successful films and albums are rarely the effort of one individual. They result from diverse talents coming together to mold the final product. This environment nurtures a culture of open communication and trust, where ideas are freely exchanged and improved upon. Realizing the importance of these collaborative dynamics, businesses and leaders can implement similar frameworks where team voices are not only heard but are integral to decision-making processes.

Another prominent technique from these industries is the acceptance of uncertainty. Creatives often work with incomplete information, trusting their intuition and experience to fill in the gaps. In the world of film, for instance, directors might not know how audiences will react until the first screening. They must decide which elements will resonate and which will not, often using their past experiences and creative intuition. Cultivating such intuition is valuable in high-stakes settings, where not every variable can be anticipated. It's about weighing available evidence, leaning on past insights, and being comfortable with the unknown.

Risk-taking stands at the heart of creative ventures. Whether it's a fashion designer debuting a daring new style or a startup trying a bold marketing approach, willingness to take risks can spur innovation and drive success. It's essential to recognize that not every risk pays off, but those that do often redefine the market or create new trends. Applying this mindset in other fields requires a delicate balance between calculated risk and foresight. Decision-makers can learn to gauge potential rewards against the backdrop of uncertainty, understanding that sometimes, the most unconventional choices can yield the greatest benefits.

Empathy is another cornerstone of creative industries that holds tremendous potential when applied to decision-making. Creatives often design or perform with their audience in mind, crafting experiences that resonate emotionally. In business contexts, empathic decision-making involves putting oneself in the stakeholders' shoes, understanding their needs, and predicting how decisions will impact them. This perspective can lead to more inclusive and effective decisions that foster goodwill and build lasting relationships.

Scenario planning is a practice frequently observed amongst creatives, particularly in gaming and storytelling. Writers and directors map out different narratives and potential outcomes, often working backwards to understand what actions lead to a desired conclusion. This kind of strategic foresight can be a powerful tool when making decisions in unpredictable environments. Professionals can use this technique to visualize potential paths, assess their implications, and prepare contingency plans.

Reflection is also a vital component of the creative process. Artists regularly review their work, seeking feedback and staying open to critique. This reflects a commitment to constant improvement and learning from mistakes. Incorporating regular reflection sessions after key decisions can help professionals identify what worked well and what didn't, paving the way for better decisions in the future. It echoes a principle that creativity doesn't end with action; it's a continuous loop of learning, adapting, and reimagining.

Lastly, the power of storytelling cannot be underestimated. Creatives are masters of crafting narratives that captivate and persuade. In the business world, telling a compelling story can be the difference between a groundbreaking decision that garners support and an overlooked opportunity. Storytelling in decision-making involves clearly articulating the vision behind choices, highlighting the values and goals they intend to achieve, and inspiring others to share in that vision.

As you navigate high-pressure situations, consider these techniques from creative industries. Embrace iteration, collaboration, and risk-taking while staying open to intuition and empathy. Use scenario planning to strategically foresee outcomes and regularly reflect to foster continuous improvement. By adopting these creative strategies, you can transform decision-making challenges into opportunities, harnessing the power of creativity to make informed and confident choices.

Chapter 24: Enhancing Decision-Making Skills

To truly enhance your decision-making skills, it's essential to adopt a mindset of ongoing growth and refinement. The cornerstone of improvement lies in continuous learning, which involves actively seeking out new knowledge and experiences, thereby broadening your understanding of diverse situations. By embracing this approach, you'll consistently sharpen your ability to evaluate options and foresee potential outcomes with greater clarity. Additionally, developing a personal development plan tailored to your unique goals ensures you remain on a trajectory towards excellence. Such a plan might include setting specific, measurable objectives and regularly reviewing your progress, helping maintain focus and motivation. Remember, the journey to enhancing your decision-making skills is not a destination but a conscious, evolving effort to adapt and thrive in the face of ever-growing challenges and opportunities. Cultivating this dynamic process will empower you to make more informed and confident choices, effectively turning pressure into a pathway for success.

Continuous Learning and Improvement

When navigating the complex landscape of high-stakes decisions, what separates exceptional decision-makers from the rest is their commitment to continuous learning and improvement. In a rapidly changing world, the skills that served us well yesterday may not suffice tomorrow. This calls for a mindset geared toward perpetual growth. Every decision, successful or otherwise, serves as a stepping stone to better understanding how we can hone our judgment.

Continuous learning starts with the cultivation of curiosity. Embrace it as a vehicle to explore the unknown and challenge assumptions. Curiosity not only broadens our knowledge base but also enhances our ability to empathize and connect with diverse perspectives. By regularly immersing ourselves in new domains, whether through books, courses, or conversations with experts, we maintain a dynamic understanding of the world around us. This isn't merely an intellectual exercise; it's a vital component of practical decision-making competence.

An effective decision-maker isn't just reactive. They actively seek feedback and use it as fuel for improvement. This often involves embracing a level of humility—recognizing that no decision is perfect and accepting constructive criticism graciously. Whether feedback comes from peers, stakeholders, or even retrospective self-reflection, it provides invaluable insights that can refine future decision-making processes. It's about cultivating an iterative loop where each decision informs the next, creating a robust cycle of improvement.

Despite the best efforts to learn and grow, missteps are inevitable. Rather than viewing mistakes as failures, they're crucial opportunities for learning. Post-decision analysis allows us to dissect outcomes, evaluate the factors that influenced results, and adjust our approaches accordingly. This process isn't confined to negative outcomes; analyzing successful decisions is equally important. Understanding why things went right can solidify effective strategies and reinforce successful behaviors.

Adopting a growth mindset is fundamental to continuous improvement. Carol Dweck's seminal work highlights the power of believing one's abilities can be developed through hard work and dedication. A growth mindset fosters resilience and adaptability, essential traits for anyone frequently engaging in high-pressure decision-making. It alleviates the fear of failure and encourages experimentation, motivating individuals to push beyond their comfort zones and explore innovative paths.

Another critical aspect of continual learning is the enhancement of emotional intelligence. Emotional awareness helps in controlling stress and making rational decisions when under duress. By working on skills such as self-regulation, empathy, and relationship management, decision-makers can better navigate the interpersonal dynamics that often accompany high-stakes scenarios. Emotional intelligence is not a static ability; it improves with practice, feedback, and deliberate reflection.

Building collaborative networks offers dual benefits. It expands knowledge by exposing decision-makers to different expertise and viewpoints, and it creates a support system that makes learning opportunities more accessible. Being part of a vibrant community of like-minded professionals encourages sharing best practices and learning from each other's experiences. Collaboration doesn't just enhance individual skills; it improves the collective decision-making capacity of the group.

Technological advancements offer tools that facilitate continuous learning. Online platforms and interactive tools provide valuable resources for those eager to stay ahead. Technologies like AI-powered analytics and data visualization can help decision-makers understand complex environments more intuitively. Staying updated with such tools enhances one's ability to make informed choices quickly and effectively. However, it's equally important to understand the limitations of technology and remain the critical thinker behind the machine.

The key to continuous learning is not just acquiring new skills but understanding how and when to employ them. This involves a degree of personalization. Each professional faces unique challenges and must tailor their learning and improvement strategies accordingly. What works for one individual or in one industry might not be effective elsewhere. Identifying and focusing on areas that align with personal and professional goals ensures that efforts in continuous learning yield meaningful results.

Finally, embedding a culture of learning within organizations amplifies individual efforts and maximizes the overall impact. When organizations value development and create environments where learning is encouraged, individuals feel empowered to pursue growth without fearing the repercussions of temporary setbacks. This culture can propel collective progress, leading to more agile and informed organizational decision-making.

Embarking on a journey of continuous learning and improvement requires commitment and patience. The landscape of high-pressure decision-making is fraught with challenges, yet equally ripe with opportunities for development and transformation. By embracing this pursuit, we equip ourselves—and those around us—to meet the most daunting challenges head-on with confidence and clarity.

Building a Personal Development Plan

Building a personal development plan tailored to enhancing decision-making skills is akin to crafting a blueprint for one's growth. It's a strategic endeavor that requires careful consideration of one's strengths, weaknesses, and aspirations. At its core, this plan acts as a roadmap, providing direction and focus in the pursuit of becoming a more proficient decision-maker, especially in high-stakes environments.

The first step in crafting a personal development plan for decision-making is introspection. Begin by assessing your current decision-making abilities and identifying the areas that require improvement. Are you prone to decision paralysis, or do you find yourself acting impulsively without fully understanding the consequences? Understanding these aspects will guide you in setting specific, measurable goals that are both ambitious and attainable.

Once you've identified key areas for improvement, it's important to set clear and actionable goals. Goals should be framed in a way that motivates you to aim higher while still being realistic. For instance, if you're a manager who often struggles with delegating tasks, a goal might be to develop a delegation framework that ensures the right tasks are assigned to the right team members. This approach not only benefits your decision-making but also enhances team productivity.

As you develop your plan, consider incorporating strategies and techniques that are aligned with your learning style. Some individuals thrive on structured learning environments, benefitting from courses and workshops that provide comprehensive decision-making frameworks. Others may prefer experiential learning through mentorship or role-playing scenarios that mimic real-world pressure situations. Embrace what works best for you, continuously testing and refining these strategies to see the maximum benefit.

Feedback loops are essential in the personal development journey, particularly for decision-making skills. Constructive feedback from peers, mentors, or coaches can offer valuable insights into your decision-making processes and outcomes. It fosters an environment of continuous improvement where you are open to recognizing missteps and eager to adapt. Be proactive in seeking out this feedback, and use it to iterate on your plan as you progress.

In building your plan, cultivating self-awareness cannot be overstated. Self-awareness involves a deep understanding of how your emotions and cognitive biases can influence decision-making. It acts as a safeguard, ensuring that decisions are not clouded by momentary feelings or ingrained biases. Techniques such as mindfulness and reflective journaling can bolster self-awareness, keeping you aligned with your core values and principles.

The integration of stress management techniques into your personal development plan also holds incredible promise. High-pressure decisions often lead to stress, which can impair judgment and lead to suboptimal outcomes. Cultivating stress resilience through practices such as mindfulness meditation, regular exercise, or even simple breathing exercises can aid in maintaining clarity and focus when you're under pressure.

Engage with a community of like-minded individuals who share a passion for improving decision-making skills. Joining professional groups or forums can provide access to diverse perspectives and experiences. As you interact with peers, you'll gain insights and strategies that you can incorporate into your plan, ultimately improving your decision-making acumen. This shared journey can be both inspiring and instructive, as the collective wisdom amplifies individual growth.

Your personal development plan should also involve continuous learning—a commitment to staying abreast with the latest research, tools, and methods in decision-making. Books, articles, webinars, and workshops offer abundant resources. Curate a learning portfolio that spans various subjects, from psychology to technology, ensuring a well-rounded approach to decision-making enhancement.

Remember, building a personal development plan is just the beginning; it's a living document that evolves as you progress. Regular reviews of your plan are essential. Set aside time to reflect on the progress made and any challenges faced. Adapt your goals and strategies as needed, keeping them relevant to your current circumstances and future ambitions.

Lastly, celebrate your milestones, no matter how small. Recognizing and rewarding your achievements fosters motivation and reinforces your commitment to the journey. This positive reinforcement cultivates an environment where continuous growth is not only possible but is actively pursued.

In conclusion, building a personal development plan focused on enhancing your decision-making skills is an empowering exercise. It demands introspection, strategic goal-setting, and a commitment to lifelong learning and adaptation. Such a plan equips you with the tools and mindset necessary to navigate high-stakes scenarios with confidence and poise. Prepare to embark on a journey of transformation, where each decision is an opportunity to cultivate wisdom and precision.

Chapter 25: The Future of Decision-Making

The horizon of decision-making is rapidly evolving, propelled by technological advancements and an ever-increasing complexity in global dynamics. As we peer into the future, it's clear that traditional decision-making paradigms will be reshaped by emerging trends like artificial intelligence, machine learning, and big data analytics. These innovations promise to augment our cognitive capabilities, offering us deeper insights and predictive power. However, the human element—our intuition, ethical considerations, and emotional intelligence—will remain irreplaceable, serving as a compass in navigating these tools with wisdom and integrity. To thrive in this brave new world, professionals must not only embrace these forward-thinking technologies but also prepare to tackle next-generation challenges with a blend of agility and moral clarity. The true art will lie in harmonizing human intuition with machine precision, fostering a decision-making landscape that prioritizes both innovation and humanity.

Emerging Trends and Innovations

In a world that's rapidly evolving, the landscape of decision-making is undergoing transformative changes. As we stand on the brink of these new horizons, it's crucial to understand how emerging trends and innovations shape our ability to make smarter, faster, and more informed decisions. Traditional approaches are being augmented by cutting-edge technologies and novel methodologies, offering unprecedented opportunities and challenges.

One of the most significant trends is the integration of artificial intelligence (AI) in decision-making processes. AI has the potential to revolutionize how decisions are made by offering data-driven insights and predictive analytics that go far beyond human capabilities. Machine learning algorithms can identify patterns in vast datasets, providing decision-makers with clearer foresight into potential outcomes. This doesn't just mean making decisions faster; it means making them with a higher degree of accuracy and confidence.

Imagine having a virtual assistant that sifts through mountains of data to highlight the most critical information, essentially doing the heavy lifting. This doesn't replace human intuition but rather complements it, allowing leaders to focus on strategic thinking. The synergy between human judgment and AI-driven insights can lead to revolutionary ways to tackle complex problems, especially in high-pressure situations where time and stakes are high.

However, with new technology comes the imperative to manage and mitigate risks associated with it. The ethical use of AI and privacy concerns must be factored into any decision-making framework. As professionals, ensuring that AI systems are transparent and equitable is paramount. Equipping teams with the skills necessary to critically assess AI recommendations is a step towards a resilient decision-making ecosystem.

Another trend gaining momentum is the application of behavioral economics in decision-making. By understanding the psychological factors that influence decisions, leaders can develop strategies that consider human behavior's nuanced complexities. This approach enables organizations to craft environments that lead to more rational decision-making, mitigating biases that often derail the process.

While purely analytical or economic models might fail to account for the unpredictability of human behavior, combining behavioral insights with traditional data can offer a richer view. Emerging strategies that embrace this fusion have shown particular efficacy in areas like consumer behavior, policy making, and internal corporate strategies. It's a reminder that beneath the mountain of data are people with emotions, biases, and unique thought processes.

In tandem with the psychological aspect is the increasing focus on collaboration facilitated through digital tools. Innovative platforms are emerging that allow for real-time collaboration and visualization, making it possible to bring diverse perspectives into play regardless of geographical boundaries. When each voice is heard and respected, teams become more agile and adaptable in their decision-making.

Imagine a dynamic meeting room, where decisions are informed not just by those physically present, but by a global coalition of colleagues, each offering unique insights. By leveraging technology to foster inclusivity and diversity of thought, decision makers can build more comprehensive and resilient strategies. This distributed model of decision-making is particularly valuable in today's interconnected world, where challenges know no borders.

Furthermore, we're witnessing an increased emphasis on user-centric design in decision-making tools. Businesses and technologies that put users first are transforming the decision-making landscape. Intuitive interfaces, personalized insights, and user-friendly analytics are helping even the least tech-savvy professionals harness complex technologies to their advantage. This trend signifies a move toward democratizing decision-making tools, not limiting them to experts alone.

For individuals and organizations, this means greater autonomy and empowerment. Not everyone has the resources to consult a data analyst or strategic consultant for every decision—nor should they need to. By embedding smart, user-centric design, decision-making becomes more accessible and less daunting for everyone involved.

Another key trend is the development of adaptive decision-making strategies. In an unpredictable world, flexibility is essential. Scenario planning has therefore evolved to become pivotal in strategic decision making. This involves preparing for various potential futures, encouraging decision-makers to be ready to pivot as circumstances change.

Adaptive strategies require a mindset that embraces change and uncertainty, fostering an environment where learning from mistakes isn't just accepted but anticipated. This approach supports the idea that failure is not the opposite of success, but a step on the path to achieving it. In this way, organizations can turn volatility from a threat into an opportunity.

The horizon of decision-making is bright with opportunity, albeit intertwined with challenges. By embracing AI, leveraging behavioral insights, fostering collaboration, and putting user experience at the forefront, we stand equipped to navigate whatever comes next. As we integrate these emerging trends into our decision-making processes, the key lies in maintaining a balance between technological advancement and human-centric values.

Driven by innovation and grounded in empathy, the future of decision-making calls for leaders who are not only equipped with the latest tools and techniques but are also aware of the ethical implications and responsibilities that come with them. It's an exciting time, as we witness a fundamental shift in how decisions are made and the impact they hold for our collective future.

Preparing for Next-Generation Challenges

As the landscape of decision-making continues to evolve, professionals face a plethora of new challenges that demand innovative thinking and adaptable strategies. The rapid advancement of technology, shifting global dynamics, and increased complexity in data analysis are just a few of the emerging factors transforming the way we approach high-stakes decisions. Preparing for these next-generation challenges requires a proactive mindset and a willingness to embrace change.

One of the most significant challenges is the integration of artificial intelligence and machine learning into decision-making processes. These technologies offer unprecedented opportunities to analyze data at a scale and speed previously unimaginable. However, they also present unique challenges, such as data privacy concerns and the risk of over-reliance on algorithmic suggestions. It's crucial for decision-makers to balance the insights provided by AI with human intuition and ethical considerations.

Moreover, the global business environment is becoming increasingly interconnected, with decisions made in one region having far-reaching implications worldwide. This interconnectedness necessitates a deeper understanding of cross-cultural dynamics and geopolitical factors. Decision-makers must be able to navigate these complexities with an awareness of how local actions can ripple across the globe.

Another pressing challenge is the accelerating pace of change. The speed at which industries and markets are evolving means that traditional decision-making frameworks may quickly become obsolete. To stay ahead, professionals need to develop flexible strategies that allow for rapid adaptation and continuous learning. Scenario planning and iterative decision-making models can equip leaders with the tools to pivot and respond effectively to unforeseen circumstances.

The future of decision-making will also demand heightened emotional intelligence and empathy. As the workforce becomes more diverse and inclusive, understanding and valuing different perspectives will be vital in making decisions that are not only effective but also fair and inclusive. Leaders will need to foster environments where diverse teams can contribute their insights without fear of being overshadowed.

To rise to these challenges, it's important to cultivate a decision-making culture that values transparency and accountability. Open communication and a clear alignment of values within organizations will empower individuals to make informed decisions confidently. By creating systems that encourage collaboration and trust, decision-makers can ensure that their choices are supported by a collective understanding.

It's also imperative for decision-makers to invest in continuous learning and development. The skills and knowledge that proved effective yesterday might not suffice tomorrow. By staying informed about emerging trends and innovations, professionals can remain agile and ready to capitalize on new opportunities. This means not only keeping up with industry best practices but also seeking knowledge from diverse fields and disciplines.

Furthermore, decision-making in the future will likely involve negotiating the ethical and moral implications of choices more than ever before. As technology blurs the lines between right and wrong, decision-makers need a solid ethical framework to guide their actions. Engaging in regular ethical training and discussions can help maintain a focus on integrity, even as the pressure to deliver results mounts.

Taking calculated risks will remain a cornerstone of decision-making. However, the nature of these risks will continue to evolve. Decision-makers must be adept at evaluating the potential impacts of their choices across multiple dimensions, including economic, social, and environmental factors. This holistic approach to risk assessment will be crucial as stakeholders demand more accountability and transparency.

The ability to predict and prepare for the unpredictable will differentiate influential leaders from the rest. Scenario planning, adaptive strategies, and robust crisis management plans can help cushion the impact of unforeseen disruptions. By anticipating potential challenges and having frameworks in place, decision-makers can navigate uncertainty with greater confidence.

As each of these challenges comes into clearer focus, the need to develop a personal decision-making philosophy that values both logic and intuition will become increasingly significant. It requires an openness to new ideas and a commitment to personal growth. By staying curious and embracing a mindset of lifelong learning, individuals can enhance their ability to face the future with resilience and assurance.

The next generation of decision-makers will embody a blend of technological savvy and human insight. They will navigate complexity not by shying away from it but by understanding and leveraging it. By cultivating these skills and attitudes, professionals can ensure they are well-prepared to meet the demands of the future and thrive in a rapidly evolving world.

In conclusion, preparing for next-generation challenges isn't just about adopting the latest tools or theories. It's about a comprehensive shift in mindset—a transition toward embracing complexity and leveraging it to make smarter, more informed decisions. By doing so, today's professionals can become adept leaders of tomorrow, capable of shaping the future rather than just reacting to it.

Chapter 26: Cultivating a Decision-Maker's Mindset

In the realm of high-stakes decision-making, cultivating the right mindset stands as the cornerstone of success. It's about embracing change, acknowledging uncertainty, and nurturing a sense of adaptability that helps you pivot with confidence. Imagine being not just prepared for what's expected but agile enough to face the unpredictable head-on. By intentionally refining your approach, honing both analytical and intuitive skills, you become more than a decision-maker; you transform into a strategic thinker. This involves internalizing the principle that every decision is a balance beam, weighing immediate needs against long-term outcomes and potential risks against anticipated rewards. It also means fostering resilience—treating setbacks as lessons rather than failures—and actively seeking growth through continuous learning. A decision-maker's mindset isn't static; it's an evolving trait shaped by experience, reflection, and the courage to question assumptions. Harnessing such qualities, you empower yourself to make informed choices under pressure, charting a path that reflects both wisdom and vision.

Embracing Change and Uncertainty

In the ever-evolving landscape of high-stakes decision-making, the ability to embrace change and uncertainty is not just advantageous—it's essential. For professionals tasked with navigating complex environments, the unpredictability of circumstances often presents both significant challenges and opportunities for growth. Embracing change and uncertainty demands a mindset that appreciates the fluid nature of the modern world, where unforeseen events aren't just possible but probable.

So, why is it that some decision-makers thrive in these volatile conditions while others falter? It essentially boils down to their attitude toward uncertainty and their readiness to adapt. Those who can pivot and remain adaptable in the face of sudden shifts exhibit a trait known as "adaptability quotient." It's the ability to manage unknowns effectively and still make informed decisions swiftly. Decision-makers with high adaptability quotients don't just react—they anticipate and prepare, turning potential threats into strategic opportunities.

At the core of adapting to uncertainty is the concept of mental flexibility. This involves an openness to restructure one's thoughts and to consider a variety of possibilities. Mental flexibility enables you to view challenges from multiple perspectives. It's about letting go of rigid thinking patterns and acknowledging that there are often multiple paths to a solution. A flexible mindset empowers decision-makers to pivot strategies and experiment with alternatives without fear of failure. Instead of sticking to a pre-determined plan, there's an appreciation of the importance of improvisation and innovation.

One might wonder how to cultivate such flexibility. A crucial step is developing a habit of reflective thinking. This means taking the time to evaluate past decisions, especially those made under pressure, and recognizing the lessons they impart. Each decision, whether successful or not, offers invaluable insights. Reflective thinking encourages a learning mindset that thrives on feedback and adjustments, rather than one that is bogged down by perfectionism or fear of making mistakes.

Another key element is resilience. The journey of embracing change is fraught with setbacks and imperfections. Resilient decision-makers carry forward without succumbing to the weight of past mistakes. They possess the courage to make decisions, even when outcomes are not fully assured, and to learn from each one, turning each moment of uncertainty into a stepping stone toward mastery. Building resilience involves cultivating a positive attitude towards failure, seeing it as a pivotal component of the learning process. Each setback is a teacher, guiding the way to smarter, more nuanced decision-making.

In today's dynamic business environment, decision-makers often face what feels like insurmountable ambiguity. Here, the power of perspective becomes a game-changer. Developing the ability to look at situations from multiple angles can reveal hidden opportunities within challenges. Decision-makers who eagerly weigh diverse perspectives are better equipped to deal with uncertainty because they build a more comprehensive understanding of their situations. This holistic view can expose new paths and solutions, turning what initially appeared as constraints into catalysts for innovation.

Leading with clarity amidst chaos is no small feat. Communicating effectively in uncertain times ensures that teams remain engaged and aligned with organizational goals, even when the destination is still unfocused. When leaders distill complex situations into clear, actionable insights, they enable those around them to act with confidence, reducing the paralysis of uncertainty. Clear communication instills trust and provides direction. It's about keeping everyone motivated and informed, even when the journey ahead is unfathomable.

Despite the challenges, embracing uncertainty fuels creativity. Apparently chaotic situations can break conventional thinking patterns, urging us to break free from the confines of routine and contemplate innovative strategies. Unresolved problems beg for novel solutions, urging the creative mind to surface unprecedented ideas, breaking the boundaries of traditional thought processes. The innovators and pioneers who redefine industries are often those who welcome the unknown with curiosity rather than fear.

Moreover, in the realm of high-stakes decision-making, relying on intuition is indispensable. When navigating uncertainty, intuition acts as the bridge connecting analytical assessments with less tangible insights, derived from experience and gut feelings. Intuition is informed by an intricate blend of conscious reasoning and the subconscious processing of past experiences. While it should not operate in a vacuum, coupling intuition with data-driven insights helps in balancing instinctive responses with factual realities, leading to well-rounded decision-making.

In conclusion, embracing change and uncertainty is at the heart of cultivating a decision-maker's mindset. It's about stepping into the unknown with both courage and thoughtful preparation. By nurturing adaptability, mental flexibility, and resilience, professionals can transform unpredictability into a powerful catalyst for discovery and progress. The uncertainties of our world aren't just hurdles to be overcome; they're the arenas where true leaders rise and redefine what's possible. This mindset of openness, learning, and innovation paves the way for making impactful decisions, no matter how complex or unforeseen the circumstances may appear.

Building Confidence and Agility

In the fast-paced world of high-stakes decision-making, honing confidence and agility is as crucial as understanding the mechanics of decision processes. When the heat is on, those who excel are not necessarily those with the sharpest intellect but rather those who trust their choices and adapt swiftly. This chapter delves into the twin pillars of confidence and agility, exploring what it takes to fortify these essential traits in a decision-maker's toolkit.

Imagine standing at the crossroads of a critical decision, where every path seems fraught with risk. In these moments, confidence becomes your anchor, a force that stabilizes even when uncertainty howls like a storm around you. Building confidence isn't about eliminating doubt but learning to move forward despite it. A decision-maker doesn't hesitate out of fear or over-analysis but steps forward with conviction, cultivated through experience, preparation, and a deep understanding of their values. Confident decision-making stems from self-awareness and an unwavering belief in one's judgment and capabilities. This is not about arrogance; it's about cultivating a self-assured presence that allows one to make clear-headed decisions under pressure.

One might ask, "How does one develop such confidence?" It's not a switch that can be flipped overnight. Rather, it's a journey—a long-term investment in yourself. Start by gaining clarity on your core values and principles, as discussed earlier in the framework chapter. Knowing what you stand for and what matters most acts as a compass, guiding your decisions with authenticity and integrity. Engage in reflective practices such as journaling or meditative contemplation to deepen your understanding of these values. Over time, this self-knowledge becomes a powerful tool, giving you the confidence to make choices aligned with your true self.

But let's not forget agility—an equally vital ally in decision-making. In fluid environments where circumstances can change at a moment's notice, agility is about maintaining flexibility and being ready to pivot when new information emerges. An agile mindset embraces change, seeing it not as a disruption but as an opportunity for innovation and growth. Developing agility involves cultivating an openness to new experiences and ideas, and fostering a willingness to let go of rigid plans or preconceived notions. It's about adapting quickly without losing sight of the bigger picture.

Agility, much like confidence, is built through practice. It requires an environment that allows for experimentation and learning from failure. Look to leaders in industries like technology or the military where flexibility is not just encouraged but essential for survival. In these realms, rapid iteration, feedback loops, and adaptive thinking are ingrained into the culture. As decision-makers, drawing lessons from these sectors allows us to see how agility can be practiced daily, transforming challenges into stepping stones.

Consider the game of chess—a masterful display of both confidence and agility. A chess player operates with a clear vision yet remains constantly responsive to the opponent's moves. This balance is precisely what decision-makers need to emulate: move forward with assurance but possess the nimbleness to recalibrate strategies on the fly. The confidence to commit to a move and the agility to adjust as the game evolves is what separates the great from the good.

Both confidence and agility aren't mere traits—they're habits that can be cultivated. Start small. Make it a practice to step out of your comfort zone regularly; this doesn't mean reckless risk-taking but engaging in activities that stretch your abilities. Whether it's taking on a challenging project at work or learning a new skill, these experiences build resilience and trust in your capabilities. Such endeavors teach you that setbacks are not failures but valuable lessons—each one an opportunity to grow more agile.

Another practical way to enhance both confidence and agility is through decision simulations or case studies. These exercises can mimic high-pressure environments, providing a sandbox to practice and analyze your decision-making processes without real-world consequences. Here, you can test your ability to remain steady and adaptive under different scenarios, refining your intuition and responsiveness over time.

Furthermore, collaboration can be a powerful catalyst for confidence and agility. Working with diverse teams introduces you to different perspectives and approaches, enriching your decision-making prowess. Learning from colleagues who navigate uncertainty with ease can inspire and offer new strategies to incorporate into your own arsenal. The dynamic interplay within teams fosters a culture of trust and support, empowering everyone to venture beyond comfort zones.

As you progress along the path of cultivating your mindset, remember that confidence and agility are intertwined; each reinforces the other. Confidence in your decision-making abilities frees you from the paralysis of uncertainty, while agility ensures you can navigate whatever unpredictability life throws your way. Together, they create a foundation where decisive action and fluid adaptation coexist, enabling you to lead with clarity and strength.

In closing, the journey of building confidence and agility is deeply personal but universally essential for those seeking mastery in decision-making. By consciously working to enhance these aspects, you not only elevate your capabilities but also forge a path toward becoming a more decisive and adaptive leader. Embrace the process with patience and persistence, for it's a continuous progression toward your best self as a decision-maker.

Conclusion

As we've journeyed through the intricacies of decision-making under pressure, it's clear that the path to making sound decisions is both an art and a science. In high-stakes environments, where the margin for error is slim, the ability to make informed, confident choices can be the difference between success and failure. Empowering yourself with the skills and mindset to navigate these challenges isn't just advantageous—it's essential. Throughout this book, we've explored strategies, techniques, and psychological insights to build a robust framework for decision-making that withstands the trials of pressure.

Understanding the importance of cognitive biases and emotional intelligence in the decision-making process underlines the need for self-awareness. Recognizing our limitations, biases, and emotional responses allows us to mitigate their effects, thereby refining our judgment. When we become adept at identifying these factors, we create a space where clear, rational thought processes can lead to better outcomes. This introspection combined with a decision-making framework based on core values lays a foundation that is both sturdy and flexible, much like the roots of a well-nourished tree.

Leadership insights, whether from business, military, or creative arenas, illustrate that experience is a powerful, albeit complex, teacher. The ability to learn from those who have faced similar challenges and emerged successfully gives us a blueprint to follow, but with the crucial understanding that every decision is unique. It stresses the importance of adaptable strategies, ones that consider the nuances of each scenario while holding true to guiding principles.

Communication is another cornerstone of effective decision-making. In scenarios ripe with pressure, clear and effective communication serves as a critical tool. Whether it involves conveying intentions, understanding stakeholder concerns, or simply ensuring your team is on the same page, the power of words shouldn't be underestimated. Hand in hand with communication is time management, where the ability to prioritize and act decisively without forsaking quality is paramount. Balancing these two elements can provide a calming rhythm to the chaos of decision-making under pressure.

Stress management and resilience-building techniques equip us to maintain our composure when stakes are high. The pressure can be relentless, but approaching it with the right mindset can turn potential stress into a motivational force. Relying on data supports our decision-making arsenal, ensuring our choices are backed by rigorous analysis while being mindful of inherent limitations that might distort our understanding.

Intuition, often nurtured by experience and an intimate understanding of one's field, can be an invaluable ally. Trusting your instincts while simultaneously verifying them with logical analysis creates a synergistic approach that captures the best of both worlds. This combination serves well in ethical decision-making, where moral dilemmas often require nuanced perspectives and balancing varied interests.

Overcoming decision paralysis involves developing confidence in your choices. By understanding the roots of hesitation and building strategies to counteract the pull of over-analysis, we pave the way for decisive action. In times of crisis, being prepared with a response plan can drastically alter outcomes, making real-time problem-solving both manageable and effective.

Mistakes and failures are potent teachers. They offer insights that cannot be gleaned from success alone. By systematically analyzing past decisions, we open pathways to innovation and creativity, transforming setbacks into opportunities for growth. This resilient attitude enables decision-makers to maintain momentum even when faced with adversity.

In fostering supportive environments, teams can cultivate trust and collaboration, tapping into diverse perspectives that enrich the decision-making process. Such environments encourage accountability and instill a culture where ownership of decisions becomes second nature, simultaneously fostering personal growth and collective responsibility.

The future of decision-making presents new challenges and opportunities. Emerging trends and technologies promise to reshape how we approach problems, yet the essence of sound decision-making will remain timeless: informed judgment, adaptability, and a deep understanding of the human element. By embracing change and uncertainty, decision-makers can position themselves to tackle next-generation challenges with agility and confidence.

In conclusion, the path to becoming a master decision-maker is one of continuous learning and self-improvement. By integrating new techniques with tried-and-true principles and cultivating a mindset open to change and growth, we empower ourselves to navigate high-pressure scenarios with confidence and clarity. The journey doesn't end here—it begins anew with each decision we face. Let this book serve as a guide, a companion on the path to making decisions that count, both now and into the future.

Appendix A: Additional Resources and Tools

This appendix is packed with resources and tools to guide you in becoming a more effective decision-maker under pressure. Equipped with the right resources, you can navigate high-stakes situations with confidence and precision, leveraging your newfound skills to make informed choices swiftly and effectively.

Books and Articles

- **Thinking, Fast and Slow** by Daniel Kahneman - A deep dive into the two systems of thought that drive our decisions.

- **Blink: The Power of Thinking Without Thinking** by Malcolm Gladwell - An exploration of our ability to make rapid decisions with limited information.

- **Leaders Eat Last** by Simon Sinek - Insights into developing trust and collaboration, crucial components in decision-making.

- Articles from journals such as *Harvard Business Review* and *Psychology Today* that explore modern trends and insights in decision-making.

Online Courses

- **Cognitive Behavioral Skills for Leaders** - Offered by various platforms, focusing on improving decision-making through cognitive exercises.

- Courses on platforms like Coursera and edX covering decision science and emotional intelligence.

Podcasts and Video Content

- **The Decision Education Podcast** - Discussions on improving decision-making skills through relatable examples.

- **The Tim Ferriss Show** - Interviews with leaders who share decision-making insights and processes.

- TED Talks that explore innovative thinking and leadership decisions.

Software and Apps

- **Trello** or **Asana** - Tools to organize thoughts and prioritize decisions effectively.

- **Evernote** - For capturing and organizing decision-making ideas and resources.

- **MindMeister** - A mind mapping tool to visualize decision frameworks and strategies.

Professional Communities and Networks

- **LinkedIn Groups** - Engage with groups focused on leadership and decision-making.

- Participate in **Meetup** groups for professionals looking to refine decision-making skills.

By continually accessing these resources and tools, you'll be well-equipped to handle any high-pressure situation, armed with the knowledge and confidence required to make sound decisions. As you incorporate these aids into your routines, remember: improvement is an ongoing journey. Keep striving to enhance your skills, and stay curious about the evolving landscape of decision-making.